COMMUNICATION HACKS

Also by the Same Author

The Diary of My Love

The Journey of My Love

COMMUNICATION HACKS

QUICK WAYS TO MASTER INTERPERSONAL COMMUNICATION AND UNDERSTAND OTHERS

DEESHA SANGANI

BOLD

An imprint of
Srishti Publishers & Distributors

Srishti Publishers & Distributors
A unit of AJR Publishing LLP
212A, Peacock Lane
Shahpur Jat, New Delhi – 110 049

editorial@srishtipublishers.com

First published by Bold,
an imprint of Srishti Publishers & Distributors in 2025

10 9 8 7 6 5 4 3 2 1

Printed and bound in India.

To everyone striving to connect, inspire, and be heard. This book is dedicated to the power of words, the art of listening, and the beauty of understanding. May these hacks guide you to communicate with clarity, confidence, and compassion.

Contents

Acknowledgements

I would like to extend my deepest gratitude to everyone who played a part in bringing this book to life. First and foremost, to my family—your unwavering support and encouragement have been my constant source of strength and inspiration.

To my publisher, Arup Bose, thank you for believing in this project and helping me shape my ideas into something tangible. A special thanks to the editorial team, whose keen insights and dedication ensured this book reached its full potential.

And finally, to myself—for embracing the journey and committing to the growth that writing this book has brought.

To my close friend Shravan Samnotra, who was truly a shooting star, "Brightest yet short-lived". You have been a gem who is truly missed.

1

Why Communication Matters

Once upon a time, in the busy street of a small town snuggled between mountains and a river, there were two friends named Shirya and Arjun. Shirya was outgoing, and she had a gift for good conversation, while Arjun was someone who wouldn't open up quickly and would stay quiet and reserved; it was not that he didn't know how to express himself; it was just that he preferred to express himself through art and music.

Despite their differences, Shirya and Arjun shared a deep bond forged through years of friendship. As they travelled through life, they encountered various challenges and opportunities that tested their abilities and shaped their destinies.

Along the way, they discovered the importance of communication skills in every aspect of their lives.

In Personal Relationships: Communication is the key to unlocking understanding and connection. Shirya and Arjun learned this lesson firsthand when they faced a misunderstanding that threatened their strong friendship. However, through open and honest communication, they could address their concerns, express their feelings, and strengthen their bond even further.

In Professional Pursuits: In pursuing their dreams, Shirya and Arjun found themselves in the complexities of the professional world. Shirya, with her confident communication skills, excelled in her interviews, presentations to stakeholders, and networking events, which helped her get opportunities to grow in her career. Meanwhile, Arjun discovered that his ability to communicate his artistic vision and goals effectively helped him get support and recognition for his work.

In Community Engagement: Both Shirya and Arjun became active community members. They recognised the power of communication in driving positive change. Through dialogues, collaboration, and advocacy, they worked with their neighbours to address social issues, promote understanding of diverse cultures, and create a more inclusive and vibrant community for all.

In Self-Expression: Above all, Shirya and Arjun understood that communication is about conveying messages to others through writing or talking and expressing oneself authentically and confidently. Through words, art, music, or actions, they embraced communication as a tool for self-discovery, empowerment, and fulfilment.

In life's journey, communication skills are the threads that weave our experiences, relationships, and aspirations together. From personal connections to professional success, from community engagement to self-expression, effective communication is one of the cornerstones of a fulfilling and meaningful life.

As we begin this journey together, let us heed the lessons from Shirya and Arjun's story and strive to enhance our communication skills in every aspect of our lives.

In the words of Maya Angelou, "Words are things, and a small drop of ink, falling like dew upon a thought, produces that which makes thousands, perhaps millions, think." Let us channel the power of communication to inspire, connect, and transform the world around us.

A Communicator Extraordinaire

In the heart of India, among the diverse voices and bustling streets, there resides a strong leader whose words echo across the nation, inspiring millions and trillions and shaping history.

This leader is the Prime Minister of India, Narendra Modi, whose remarkable journey is the perfect example of the transformative power of communication skills in every aspect of one's life.

Modi had a gift for speech and influence from a very young age. His ability to keep a grip on his audience, with his powerful speeches and compelling narratives, earned him recognition and respect in the community. As he commenced his political journey, Modi harnessed the power of communication skills to connect with people from all walks of life, from rural villages to urban centres. To better understand how to be a good communicator like him, we must understand what makes him different.

According to John Adair, "Communication is essentially the ability of one person to make contact with another and make himself or herself understood."

Now, if a Prime Minister of a large country like India wants to be a good communicator, they must grasp the nation's nerve. They need to reach out to the highest and lowest strata of society. Modi used social media platforms like X, Facebook, and Instagram; he engaged directly with the citizens. In doing this, he connected with various sects of technologically adept people.

But there are people in India who rely solely on TV or radio. So, he reached out to them, too, through his 'Mann ki Baat.' He also encouraged people to write letters to him.

Good communicators ***always know what they want to say*** *and* ***how to tell it.***

If we go back to our previous example, the best way to talk to Arjun, who is reserved, would be in a personal setting where he feels comfortable enough to express himself. At the same time, Shirya would be okay with talking even amongst people.

Understand what would make sense with whom you wish to communicate. If your manager is reserved, wishing them a happy birthday in a group of hundred people when they want to keep that information private might not be the best idea, whereas, for someone outgoing, this would be the highlight of their day.

Communication does not merely mean telling someone a message you want to convey. Effective communication means making sure the other person understands what you mean.

More often than not, if you are not clear about your message, you will not be able to communicate effectively.

For instance, it is because of Modi's clarity of vision that he can connect with people in a way that transcends linguistic, cultural, and geographical barriers. Wearing the clothes that come from the culture of the people he meets when he greets them and talking in their native language makes him more approachable and helps him connect with his audience. This is a quality only good communicators have.

10 Practical Tips from Narendra Modi's Communication Skills:

1. **Having Clarity of Vision:** Narendra Modi's strong, determined speech regarding his vision for India's development inspires millions because PM Modi is able to communicate his vision for the people of India very clearly. *Communicate your vision with clarity and conviction.*
2. **Be Authentic:** Modi is known for his authenticity; he speaks passionately about his beliefs and values without pretending to be someone he's not. *In life, remember you should be as genuine and authentic as you can while communicating.*
3. **Adaptability:** PM Modi seamlessly transitions from formal addresses to informal interactions. *Adapt your communication style to suit different contexts and audiences.*
4. **The Art of Storytelling:** When Narendra Modi narrates stories, the audience across India easily resonates. *Storytelling is an art; we should use storytelling to make our message memorable and relatable.*
5. **Inclusivity:** Modi's emphasis on 'Sabka Saath, Sabka Vikas' not only embodies inclusivity but also evokes the feeling of being united as a nation. *Always include diverse perspectives and voices in your communication.*
6. **Confidence:** When PM Modi is addressing something, he walks up to the stage with confidence that brings a sense of pride to us. Modi's self-assurance instils confidence in his leadership—*project confidence and conviction in your ideas and decisions.*
7. **Simplicity:** Modi's use of very simple language to connect with his audience and his narrative makes his message

accessible to everyone. *Simplify complex ideas and concepts for better understanding.*

8. **Active Listening:** In any of his programs or events, observe how PM Modi actively listens to other speakers. In fact, he picks up amazing ideas and points by actively listening to other people. Modi's 'Mann Ki Baat' program demonstrates his commitment to listening to citizens. *Listen attentively to the concerns and feedback of your audience.*
9. **Resilience:** When a person who wants to bring good changes for the people of their country becomes famous, a lot of criticism gets directed toward them. Narendra Modi is no exception to this. Modi's ability to weather storms and bounce back stronger inspires resilience in others. *Stay resilient in the face of criticisms and challenges.*

The Importance of Communication Skills

Communication skills include a wide range of abilities that enable every individual to share information, ideas, and emotions effectively in various situations and settings of life. These skills are vital for success and also for fulfilment in every aspect of life, including personal relationships, professional endeavours, and public interactions.

- One of the important aspects of communication that most of us use is **verbal communication,** which involves the use of spoken words to convey messages and information. It includes components such as clarity, tone, pitch, and pacing. Strong verbal communication skills help individuals be clear about their thoughts, engage with others effectively, and express themselves with confidence and grace.

- Did you know that 80% of our communication is through body language, facial expressions, eye contact, and gestures? These aspects are part of what is called **non-verbal communication** and they play a crucial role in conveying emotions, intentions, and attitudes. Understanding and utilising nonverbal cues effectively can enhance our communication, ability to build rapport, and also facilitate better understanding between individuals.
- Listening skills are crucial to effective communication. I personally believe that if you can master listening and observing, you can solve many problems. **Active listening** includes not only listening to what others are saying but also paying proper attention to their tone and body language. This requires empathy, patience, and a willingness to understand other people's perspectives. By practising active listening, individuals can nurture stronger relationships, resolve conflicts, and build trust.
- **Written communication** is an equally important part of communication, and it includes the use of written words to communicate messages, ideas, and information. It includes everything from writing documents, emails, reports, and text messages. Did you know strong written communication skills are essential in terms of clarity, accuracy, and professionalism in both personal and professional lives? If we are clear and concise, it will help us understand, collaborate, and be productive.
- **Interpersonal communication skills** refer to the abilities that facilitate effective and meaningful interaction between individuals. They combine verbal and nonverbal communication, active listening, empathy, and conflict

resolution. Effective interpersonal communication skills are crucial in building and maintaining healthy relationships, fostering trust, and resolving conflicts constructively.

- **Presentation skills** involve the ability to deliver information or ideas to an audience in a clear, engaging, and persuasive manner, which can be achieved by a combination of words and visuals that would make the presentation most effective. The presentation should also include important aspects such as organisation, structure, visual aids, and good delivery techniques. Strong presentation skills are an essential part of effective communication, especially in the professional world, and this includes meetings, conferences, and public speaking engagements. A well-delivered presentation can captivate an audience, convey complex information in a simple and effective way, and inspire action.
- **Negotiation skills** play an important role in resolving conflicts, reaching agreements, and achieving mutually beneficial outcomes. To negotiate we would have to make best use of active listening, problem-solving, and compromise. Strong negotiation skills lets individuals talk about their interests while also considering the needs and perspectives of others. By mastering negotiation skills, individuals can navigate challenging situations, build consensus, and support collaboration.

Before we conclude, let's keep in mind that communication skills are integral assets that empower individuals to navigate any of life's challenges, build meaningful relationships, and achieve their goals. By polishing these skills and understanding their technical aspects, individuals can unlock their full potential and thrive in all aspects of life.

Impact of Communication

Effective communication skills play a vital role in the success of businesspeople worldwide, including in India. According to a study by the International Journal of Business and Management, 85% of professional success comes from having well-developed communication skills. Another study by LinkedIn found that communication-related skills, such as verbal communication and storytelling, were among the top skills that globally employers look for while hiring. Let's explore the case of a famous Indian businesswoman to understand the impact of effective communication better.

Kiran Mazumdar-Shaw is the founder and chairperson of Biocon Limited, a biotechnology company which is based in Bangalore—the IT hub of India. Mazumdar-Shaw is a leading example of a successful Indian female entrepreneur whose effective communication skills have made a significant impact on her career.

Mazumdar-Shaw is a strong woman who has the ability to communicate her vision and influence people, she has been instrumental in Biocon's growth since 1978 to one of India's leading biotechnology companies today. Her proficiency in communicating complex scientific concepts in a clear and compelling manner has not only helped her secure crucial partnerships and investments but also positioned Biocon as a global player in the biotech industry.

Through her clear communication, Mazumdar-Shaw has been able to powerfully advocate for women's participation in STEM fields and entrepreneurship in India; she has been inspiring countless aspiring businesswomen to pursue their dreams and achieve them.

Let's understand how being an effective communicator like Mazumdar-Shaw would help you to be an outstanding communicator.

What sets Mazumdar-Shaw apart is not just her vision, but her mastery of the skill of communication. By clearly conveying her ideas, she has been able to build trust, influence stakeholders, and drive her company's growth on a global scale.

As Jim Rohn wisely said, "Take advantage of every opportunity to practice your communication skills so that when important occasions arise, you will have the gift, the style, the sharpness, the clarity, and the emotions to affect other people."

By emulating her approach, you, too, can become an outstanding communicator, capable of influencing and achieving greatness in your own endeavours.

Her example displays how effective communication skills can empower Indian businesswomen to achieve remarkable success and make a lasting impact on their industries and communities.

Another Example: According to a survey conducted by Harvard Business Review, 91% of executives believe that effective communication is important for success in business.

A study done by the University of California, Los Angeles (UCLA) has found that 93% of effective communication is determined by non-verbal prompts. Deloitte conducted research that revealed that 50% lower employee turnover rates are associated with organisations that have efficient communication plans.

Mukesh Ambani, chairman and major shareholder of Reliance Industries Limited (RIL), which is one of India's largest conglomerates, is an epic example of a well-known Indian businessman who understands the importance of strong communication skills which have helped him climb up the ladder and crack toughest deals easily. Mukesh Ambani has mastered the art of communication, setting him apart from others in his field. His ability to communicate complex ideas in a simple and relatable manner has been a key factor in his success.

To stand out in one's communication, it's important to combine clarity, the right medium, and a feedback loop with your unique style. James Humes said, "The art of communication is the language of leadership." This quote encapsulates how effective communication is not just a skill but a leadership tool that can make all the difference in achieving success, as demonstrated by leaders like Mukesh Ambani.

A clear vision is the foundation of effective communication. When you know exactly what you want to achieve, it becomes easier to convey your message with precision and purpose.

Mukesh Ambani's strategic use of various communication channels has played a key role in his ability to connect with stakeholders and make critical business decisions. Choosing the right medium of communication is crucial to ensure your message is received and understood. Whether it's through a formal presentation, an email, or a face-to-face conversation, the medium you select can greatly impact the effectiveness of your communication.

2

The Fundamentals of Good Communication

Communication is the foundation of human interaction, and it defines how we carry out our relationships, professions, and personal growth. Mastering great communication skills is crucial for both professional and personal success, and fulfilment. Let's examine the fundamental elements of effective communication and explore how they apply to many aspects of life.

- **Clarity:** Clarity refers to the ability to convey messages in a clear, concise, and understandable manner. It involves using simple language, organising thoughts logically, and ensuring that the intended message is easily grasped by the audience. Clarity helps to eliminate ambiguity and confusion, making it easier for listeners or readers to comprehend and respond appropriately.

- **Adaptability:** The ability to adjust one's communication style to different situations and audiences is essential for success. Adapting to fellow workers' preferences and communication styles boosts teamwork and productivity at work. Similarly, adapting to the needs and personalities of others develops connections and promotes peace.
- **Confidence:** Confidence is crucial for effective communication because it creates trust and credibility in the speaker. In the work environment, confidence motivates colleagues and clients, allowing for better leadership and decision-making. Similarly, in interactions with others, confidence enables individuals to express themselves openly and assertively, resulting in greater self-assurance and respect from others.
- **Feedback and Reflection:** Effective communication is an ongoing process of learning and progress. Seeking feedback from others and reflecting on our own communication style allows us to discover our professional and personal strengths and leads to development.

These are all essential components of effective communication. By mastering these core abilities, people can manage the complexities of work circumstances, develop effective personal relationships, and attain their full potential in every area of life. As we embark on this path of communication mastery, remember that effective communication involves far more than simply the words we say; it is also about the connections that we establish and the impact we make on the world around us.

Communication: The Key to Connection

Communicating is more than just words—it is the link between hearts and brains. It helps in forming relationships, encouraging understanding, and moving ahead in life. In this chapter, we will go deeply into the essence of communication, discussing its definition, significance, and transforming impact in both professional and personal settings.

Communication is defined as the interchange of information, ideas, and emotions between individuals or groups. It includes verbal and non-verbal signs such as spoken words, gestures, facial expressions, and body language. Communication goes beyond language, allowing us to connect with people on a deeper, more meaningful level.

Communication plays an essential role in community engagement and creating social impact. Effective communication can inspire people, enhance awareness, and drive positive change at all stages, from grassroots movements to national movements. Whether fighting for social justice, promoting environmental sustainability, or empowering vulnerable populations, communication can serve as a catalyst for collective action and societal transformation.

Communication shifts our experiences, influences our interactions, and defines our impact on the world around us, from the boardroom to the dining table, the classroom to the streets. Let us try to nurture and enhance our ability to communicate, not only for personal growth and professional success but also for the overall benefit of mankind.

As Margaret Wheatley once said, "Without communication, there is no relationship; without respect, there is no love; without trust, there is no reason to continue." Let us embrace communication as a foundation for connection, comprehension, and harmony in our lives.

Amitabh Bachchan: A Master of Communication

Amitabh Bachchan is well-known in the Indian film industry for his exceptional communication skills. Beyond his towering presence on screen, Bachchan's ability to express himself effectively surpasses cinematic limits, leaving a lasting impression on Indian society.

Bachchan has captivated audiences with his strong voice, expressive gestures, and flawless delivery throughout his professional career. His knack for communicating, whether portraying complex characters or delivering unforgettable conversations, has propelled him to the status of cultural icon and source of inspiration for generations of performers and artists.

Nevertheless, Bachchan's communication skills extend far beyond the silver screen. In his personal life, he has demonstrated empathy, humility, and grace in his interactions with fans, fellow workers and the general public. His honest messages of solidarity during times of crisis, his genuine thoughts on life's hardships, and ongoing devotion to social concerns have gained him millions of fans and earned him recognition as a public figure.

Amitabh Bachchan stands apart from his peers through his exceptional communication skills. Bachchan's ability to convey deep emotions and complex characters has left an indelible mark on audiences and has made him a source of inspiration for generations.

Beyond his cinematic achievements, his empathy, humility, and grace in personal interactions have garnered him widespread admiration and respect.

> "Communication is the most important skill any leader can possess."
>
> —Richard Branson

Amitabh Bachchan's communication skills extend far beyond the silver screen, highlighting the importance of having a clear vision of how one conveys messages. His success can be attributed to his ability to maintain clarity of vision in his roles, ensuring that his characters and messages are delivered with precision. This clarity allows him to connect deeply with audiences, portraying complex emotions and ideas with remarkable effectiveness.

Bachchan's choice of medium—whether through his powerful voice, expressive gestures, or compelling dialogues—has played a crucial role in his success. His effective use of these mediums enhances his communication, making each performance memorable and impactful. His mastery in utilising various forms of communication underscores how adapting to different mediums can amplify the effectiveness of one's message.

Bachchan's openness to feedback and his continuous improvement are key aspects of his communication prowess. By integrating constructive criticism and evolving his approach, he has managed to stay relevant and influential throughout his career. His willingness to refine his craft demonstrates how valuable feedback is in enhancing communication skills and achieving long-term success.

Effective Communication

Communication is the hidden thread that connects us and shapes our interactions, relationships, and destiny. Like the symphony, it is comprised of different components that work together to create beautiful rhythms of understanding and connection. Now, we will look at the four major parts of effective communication—verbal, non-verbal, written, and listening skills—and discuss practical ideas for improving each in both professional and personal settings.

Verbal Communication

Verbal communication refers to the use of spoken words to express messages, ideas, and emotions. Its aspects are tone, pitch, volume, and clarity. Nirmala Sitharaman, the Finance Minister of India, is a prominent example of effective verbal communication. In her budget speeches, she articulately presents complex financial policies and economic strategies to the public and lawmakers. Her ability to explain intricate fiscal concepts in a clear and relatable manner showcases her verbal communication skills.

For instance, during her budget speech in 2021, she highlighted the government's plans for economic recovery post-COVID-19, using simple language and relatable examples to ensure that her message resonated with both the general public and experts in the field. This approach not only informs but also engages her audience, illustrating the power of verbal communication in leadership and governance.

Top 3 Frustrations:

- **Inability to Express Thoughts Clearly**: Misunderstandings arise when people find it difficult to put their ideas into words.
- **Interruptions and Over-talking**: Interrupting a discussion frequently can be annoying and make it more difficult to communicate effectively.
- **Anxiety and Nervousness**: Having anxiety or feeling uneasy when speaking can lead to stuttering and a loss of confidence.

Top 3 Fears:

- **Fear of Public Speaking**: Speaking in front of an audience can be intimidating for many people because they worry about seeming foolish, being judged, or making blunders.
- **Fear of Miscommunication**: People often experience severe anxiety when they fear that their message may be misinterpreted or not be received as intended.
- **Fear of Feedback**: People may feel reluctant to communicate when they fear they may receive unfavourable comments or criticism.

Top 3 Ways to Overcome:

- **Practice Frequently**: Having conversations and engaging in public speaking regularly will assist in developing clarity and confidence.
- **Effectively Make Use of Pauses**: Taking breaks can facilitate better thought organisation and lessen the chance of getting interrupted.
- **Seek Feedback**: Taking the initiative to look for helpful criticism will help you pinpoint your areas of weakness, and then you can improve on them and gain confidence.

Non-Verbal Communication

Virat Kohli, the renowned player and captain of India's cricket team, is a great example of non-verbal communication expertise. Kohli's tough look, confident posture, and expressive gestures inspire his squad while also terrifying opponents.

Tips for Improving Non-verbal Communication:

- Maintain eye contact to demonstrate sincerity and concentration.

- Pay attention to your body language; stand or sit straight to convey confidence.
- Mirroring other people's body language might help you create rapport and connection.

Top 3 Frustrations:

- **Misinterpreted Body Language**: When a speaker uses body language that can be misinterpreted easily, it might be unclear what their goals or sentiments are.
- **Lack of Eye Contact**: Not being able to keep eye contact can be interpreted as insecurity or indifference.
- **Uncomfortable Gestures:** Making unsuitable or too dramatic gestures can detract from the point being made.

Top 3 Fears:

- **Fear of Being Misunderstood**: The fear that miscommunication and confrontations may result from their body language or emotions.
- **Fear of Being Judged:** The worry that people would make poor assumptions about them based on non-verbal signs, like apparent anxiety or insecurity.
- **Fear of Not Being Able to Connect**: Fear that ineffective non-verbal communication would prevent them from developing deep bonds and relationships.

Top 3 Ways to Overcome:

- **Be Aware of Your Body Language**: Using open gestures and keeping eye contact are examples of positive body language that can improve communication.

- **Mirror Techniques**: Seeing others' body language and gently reflecting it back to them can help establish rapport and help ensure that communications are understood correctly.
- **Relaxation Methods**: Reduction of anxiety and enhancement of body language can be achieved by using relaxation methods like deep breathing.

Written Communication

Written communication refers to the use of words to express information, ideas, and messages. Its components are clarity, consistency, language, and style. Chetan Bhagat, bestselling novelist and columnist, is an outstanding personality in the field of written communication. Bhagat's capacity to create fascinating narratives, connect with readers, and stimulate societal conversations through his novels and essays exemplifies the power of written communication.

Tips for Improving Written Communication:

- Before you begin writing, take some time to collect your thoughts.
- To effectively communicate, use concise and clear language.
- Proofread your writing for grammatical errors and clarity.

Top 3 Frustrations:

- **Trouble Coordinating Thoughts**: Writing coherently can be difficult, resulting in messages that are not entirely clear.
- **Grammatical Errors**: Consistent spelling or grammar errors can damage credibility and professionalism.
- **Lack of Engagement**: Writing that is boring or uninteresting may not be able to hold the reader's interest.

Top 3 Fears:

- **Fear of Judgment:** Many people worry about how their writing will be perceived by others. This includes concerns about grammar, style, and the overall quality of their work. The fear of negative feedback or criticism can be paralysing.
- **Fear of Not Being Understood:** There's often anxiety about whether the message will be clear and if the audience will understand the intended meaning. Miscommunication can lead to misunderstandings, which is a significant concern for many writers.
- **Fear of Failure:** This encompasses the fear of not meeting one's own expectations or the expectations of others. It can include worries about not being able to complete a writing task successfully or not achieving the desired outcome.

Top 3 Ways to Overcome:

- **Plan Before Writing**: Making an outline before starting a piece of writing might aid in maintaining clarity and organising ideas.
- **Edit and Proofread**: Correcting typos in written communication can enhance professionalism and make it easier to read.
- **Engage the Reader**: Written communication can be made more interactive and intriguing by using questioning, storytelling strategies, and engaging language.

Listening Skills

Listening skills comprise actively absorbing and understanding both verbal and non-verbal messages from others. It includes empathy, attention, patience, and feedback. Dr APJ Abdul Kalam, India's former President and famous scientist, exhibited the mastery of listening abilities. Dr Kalam's humble attitude, genuine interest in other people's points of view, and capacity to listen without judgment made him popular with people from all walks of life.

Tips for Improving Listening Skills:

- Focus on the speaker and eliminate distractions when practising active listening.
- Ask clarifying questions to ensure that you understand and to show interest.
- Provide suggestions and validation to show that you heard and accepted the speaker's message.

Top 3 Frustrations

- **Distractions**: It's possible to miss important information if you are easily distracted and don't pay close attention to the speaker.
- **Prejudice**: Having preconceived notions before paying attention to what the speaker has to say might cause misconceptions and prejudiced answers.
- **Poor Retention**: Effective communication and follow-up can be impeded by trouble in recalling what was said.

Top 3 Fears:

- **Fear of Misunderstanding:** Many people worry that they might not fully understand what the speaker is trying to convey. This fear can stem from concerns about missing important details or misinterpreting the message.
- **Fear of Judgment:** Similar to written communication, there's a fear of being judged for one's listening abilities.

People might worry that they will be perceived as inattentive, uninterested, or incapable of understanding complex information.

- **Fear of Emotional Impact:** Listening can sometimes involve hearing difficult or emotional content. The fear of being emotionally affected by what is heard or not knowing how to respond appropriately can be a significant barrier.

Top 3 Ways to Overcome

- **Active Listening Strategies**: Using strategies like summarising and posing questions can help with comprehension and recall.
- **Reduce Distractions**: Listening abilities can be improved by establishing a concentrated setting and reducing distractions.
- **Maintain an Open Mind**: Refraining from making assumptions and maintaining an open mind can enhance listening skills and result in deeper conversations.

Key Takeaways

Successful communication is the golden thread in the symphony of human interaction, connecting people, encouraging understanding, and accelerating development. Mastering the elements of verbal, non-verbal, written, and listening abilities allows us to deal with every aspect of professional and personal life with confidence and grace. As we are influenced by Amitabh Bachchan, Virat Kohli, Chetan Bhagat, and Dr APJ Abdul Kalam's outstanding ability to communicate, let us strive for excellence in our own communication abilities and maximise the full potential of our interpersonal connections and endeavours. To summarise:

- Clarity of vision in communication is essential for effectively conveying your ideas and intentions. When you have a clear understanding of your goals and message, it becomes easier to articulate your thoughts in a way that resonates with your audience. This clarity helps you stay focused, prevents misunderstandings, and ensures that your communication is impactful and purposeful.
- Choosing the right medium of communication—verbal, non-verbal, written, or listening—depends on the context and your audience. Each medium has its strengths and can enhance your message in different ways. For example, verbal communication is ideal for real-time conversations and presentations, while written communication is best for detailed explanations and documentation. Non-verbal cues can reinforce or contradict verbal messages, and active listening ensures you fully understand and respond appropriately.
- Providing constructive feedback is a crucial aspect of effective communication. It helps individuals improve by highlighting areas for growth and reinforcing positive behaviours. When giving feedback, ensure it is clear, specific, and delivered in a supportive manner. This helps the recipient understand how to improve and fosters a culture of open communication and continuous development.

3

Communication: A Startup Game-Changer

In the fast-paced start-up industry, effective communication is the foundation for success. From selling ideas to investors to encouraging team collaboration, communicating effectively and empathetically is critical for navigating the ever-changing entrepreneurship landscape.

Let's look at the stories of two important personalities in India's start-up ecosystem which demonstrate the transforming power of communication:

Ritesh Agarwal: Mastering the Pitch

Ritesh Agarwal, the founder and CEO of OYO Rooms, set out to transform the Indian hotel business. His success depended on his ability to articulate his vision with passion, clarity, and conviction.

In constant pitching discussions with investors, Agarwal described OYO Rooms as a disruptor prepared to change how people travel and stay. Agarwal acquired the funds and support needed to grow OYO Rooms into a worldwide powerhouse by using captivating storytelling and his in-depth knowledge of industry dynamics.

His ability to articulate this vision with passion, clarity, and conviction was crucial to his success. By clearly communicating his goals and the potential impact of OYO Rooms, Agarwal was able to align his team, attract investors, and build a strong brand identity. Clarity of vision allowed him to inspire others and gain the support needed to turn his dream into reality.

In his constant pitching discussions with investors, Agarwal effectively utilised various mediums of communication. Whether through face-to-face meetings, detailed presentations, or engaging digital content, he consistently conveyed OYO Rooms' mission as a disruptor in the travel and hospitality industry. Agarwal understood the importance of choosing the right medium for each audience, ensuring that his message was not only heard but also understood and embraced by all stakeholders.

Agarwal's success was also rooted in his ability to seek and provide feedback. He actively listened to the concerns and suggestions of investors, employees, and customers, using this feedback to refine OYO Rooms' offerings and operations. By maintaining open lines of communication and fostering a culture of continuous improvement, Agarwal ensured that OYO Rooms remained responsive to the market's needs and poised for growth.

> "Effective communication is 20% what you know and 80% how you feel about what you know."
>
> —Jim Rohn

Falguni Nayar: Developing Nykaa

Falguni Nayar is an important source of inspiration for future entrepreneurs in the e-commerce industry. Nayar, the founder and CEO of Nykaa, transformed India's beauty and wellness market with her innovative online platform.

Nayar's outstanding communication abilities were key to Nykaa's success, enabling her to establish a loyal customer base and a strong brand identity. Through engaging content, personal customer interactions, and creative marketing campaigns, Nayar effectively presented Nykaa's dedication to excellence, diversity, and inclusivity, earning millions of customers' trust and commitment across the country.

Her vision wasn't just about selling products; it was about creating an experience that resonated with millions. This clarity of purpose allowed her to communicate effectively with her team, partners, and customers, ensuring everyone was aligned with Nykaa's mission. By consistently articulating her vision, Nayar was able to build a strong brand that stood out in a competitive market.

The choice of communication medium played a crucial role in Nykaa's success. Nayar understood that reaching her target audience required a strategic blend of digital and traditional communication channels. She leveraged social media, email marketing, and content-driven campaigns to engage with customers online while also utilising offline events and collaborations to create a holistic brand experience. Nayar's ability to choose the right mediums ensured that Nykaa's message of quality, inclusivity, and customer satisfaction was consistently delivered, helping in building a loyal customer base and a recognisable brand identity.

By fostering a culture of open communication within her team, Nayar ensured that ideas could flow freely and that challenges could be addressed promptly. She also valued customer feedback, using it to refine products, improve services, and enhance the overall customer experience. This continuous loop of feedback allowed Nykaa to stay agile, responsive and aligned with customer needs, further solidifying its position.

She actively sought input from customers, employees, and industry experts to refine Nykaa's offerings and customer experience. By valuing and acting on feedback, Nayar ensured that Nykaa remained responsive to customer needs and market trends. This open communication loop helped Nykaa to adapt, innovate, and maintain its leading position in the e-commerce industry.

Falguni Nayar's outstanding communication skills have been pivotal to Nykaa's growth and success. Her ability to clearly articulate her vision, choose the right medium of communication, and leverage feedback has set her apart as an inspirational leader in the e-commerce industry. Future entrepreneurs can learn from Nayar's example by developing strong communication skills that not only build a brand but also foster lasting customer relationships.

> "The most important thing in communication is hearing what isn't said."
>
> —Peter Drucker

Practical Tips from Ritesh Agarwal and Falguni Nayar

- ***Create a Compelling Narrative***: Whether you're pitching investors or engaging customers, storytelling is a great way to capture people's attention and communicate your ideas.

- ***Listen to Feedback***: Actively seek feedback from consumers, investors, and team members to improve your ideas and create successful strategies.
- ***Develop Relationships:*** Build positive relationships with all parties involved through open communication, transparency, and sincerity.
- ***Adaptability is Essential***: Make your communication strategy flexible and adaptable to meet your objectives—so you can face unseen challenges and grasp new opportunities with efficiency.
- ***Invest in Your Team***: Encourage open communication and collaboration within your start-up team, encouraging everyone to share their unique perspectives and talents.
- ***Communicate Your Opinions***: Communicate your opinions by aligning your message with your start-up's core values and mission, creating a compelling story that resonates with stakeholders.
- ***Embrace Digital Platforms***: Use digital communication tools and platforms to reach a larger audience, connect with customers, and boost engagement.
- ***Empathy***: Understand your target audience's needs and perspectives, then tailor your communication to make meaningful connections and increase engagement.
- ***Be authentic:*** Communicate in a true and sincere manner, establishing trust and credibility with stakeholders.
- ***Celebrate Success***: Share milestones and celebrate victories with your team and stakeholders to generate a sense of

pride and cooperation and the motivation to keep striving for excellence.

Effective communication is more than a skill in today's dynamic and competitive start-up environment; it is a strategic requirement. Entrepreneurs like Ritesh Agarwal and Falguni Nayar have not only achieved remarkable success by mastering the art of communication, but they have also inspired a new generation of innovators to capitalise on communication to drive positive change and create a brighter future for India's start-up ecosystem.

As we embark on our own entrepreneurial journeys, let us take note of their lessons and insights, trying to communicate with clarity, authenticity, and empathy as we navigate the exciting opportunities and obstacles that await us.

Communication is more than just a way for sharing information—in the fast-paced world of start-ups, it is the lifeline that connects entrepreneurs to their teams, investors, consumers, and the ecosystem as a whole. However, start-up owners have particular difficulties with communication that can make or kill their business ventures.

Vijay Shekhar Sharma: Founder of Paytm

Vijay Shekhar Sharma, the visionary behind India's top digital payment network, had various communication challenges on his journey to success. Sharma's journey, from putting forward his idea to reluctant financiers to expressing the value proposal of digital payments to a varied audience, shows the importance of clarity, persuasion, and adaptability in communication.

One of the most significant hurdles was conveying his ground-breaking idea to financiers who were initially reluctant to back the concept of digital payments in India. Sharma had to communicate his vision with remarkable clarity and conviction, ensuring that potential investors could see the untapped potential in a market that was still heavily reliant on cash transactions. His ability to articulate the value of digital payments, despite scepticism, played a crucial role in securing the funding that helped turn Paytm into a household name.

Sharma needed to tailor his message to resonate with different groups—from tech-savvy millennials to small business owners and even traditional consumers who were wary of moving away from cash. His ability to adapt his communication style based on the audience's needs and concerns was essential in driving the widespread adoption of Paytm across various demographics. Through clear, persuasive, and adaptable communication, Sharma not only built trust in Paytm's services but also educated the public about the benefits of digital payments.

The communication skills Sharma honed throughout his journey were pivotal in Paytm's rapid growth and success. His clarity in presenting complex ideas, persuasive abilities in winning over sceptics, and adaptability in addressing diverse audiences allowed him to break down barriers and build a network that millions of Indians now rely on for their daily transactions. Sharma's effective communication was not just about selling an idea—it was about creating a movement that transformed the way India handles money.

Practical Skills

Enhancing Persuasion Skills: Developing the ability to clearly and persuasively communicate your ideas can help you influence decisions and bring others on board with your vision, whether in a personal or professional setting.

Adapting to Diverse Audiences: Learning to adapt your communication style based on your audience ensures that your message is understood and well-received by people from different backgrounds, making interactions smoother and more effective.

Shradha Sharma: Founder of Your Story

Shradha Sharma, the founder of Your Story, India's premier media platform for start-ups and entrepreneurs, successfully navigated the challenging environment of storytelling and communication. Sharma's communication abilities were important in creating a healthy community and amplifying the voices of Indian companies—from interviewing founders to choosing material that resonated with a wide audience.

Her vision for creating a platform dedicated to start-ups and entrepreneurs was unique, and she faced the daunting challenge of carving out a niche in a competitive environment. Sharma's exceptional communication skills played a crucial role in this endeavour. She understood the power of storytelling and leveraged it to highlight the journeys of countless entrepreneurs, bringing their stories to the forefront of India's business ecosystem. Her ability to connect deeply with her interview subjects and audience allowed her to create content that resonated widely, making Your Story a go-to platform for inspiring entrepreneurial tales.

Sharma's communication abilities extended beyond just storytelling; she was instrumental in building a vibrant community of entrepreneurs, investors, and innovators. By carefully selecting content that spoke to the aspirations and challenges of Indian start-ups, Sharma fostered a sense of belonging and support among her readers. Her interviews with founders were not just conversations but insightful dialogues that amplified the voices of Indian entrepreneurs. This community-building aspect of Your Story, driven by Sharma's empathetic and engaging communication style, has been vital in creating a supportive environment where start-ups can thrive.

Shradha Sharma's communication skills have been key to Your Story's growth and success. By consistently delivering content that resonates with a wide audience, Sharma has built a loyal following and established Your Story as a trusted source of entrepreneurial inspiration. Her ability to tell compelling stories and create meaningful connections with her audience has not only expanded Your Story's reach but also solidified its position as India's premier media platform for start-ups.

Power Up Your Communication Skills

Building Stronger Relationships: Just as Sharma built a thriving community around Your Story, effective communication can help you foster deeper connections with people in your personal and professional life. By listening actively and speaking empathetically, you can create trust and mutual respect.

Enhancing Persuasion and Influence: Sharma's success in making Your Story a leading platform was largely due to her ability to persuade and inspire through her storytelling. In everyday life, strong communication skills can help you articulate your ideas more clearly, making it easier to persuade others and influence positive outcomes.

Unique Communication Challenges Faced by Start-Up Founders

1. **Navigating Uncertainty:** Start-up founders frequently find themselves in unexpected scenarios, experiencing uncertainty and ambiguity at every turn. Effective communication in such unpredictable circumstances necessitates clarity, honesty, and the capacity to instil trust in the face of uncertainty.
2. **Establishing credibility and trust** is crucial for business owners, particularly when pitching ideas to investors, acquiring top talent, or bringing in customers. Effective communication, backed up by evidence, testimonials, and an interesting story, may help founders build credibility and trust.
3. **Managing Stakeholder Expectations:** Start-up founders must manage the expectations of various stakeholders, including investors, employees, customers, and partners. Balancing these various aims necessitates good communication skills such as active listening, empathy, and diplomacy.
4. **Crisis Communication:** In the ever-changing world of start-ups, crises are inescapable. Whether it's a product failure, a public relations disaster, or a circumstance of change in leadership, entrepreneurs' ability to communicate during crises can make or destroy their brand and reliability. Timely, transparent, and empathic communication is essential for repairing damage and restoring trust.

Practical Tips from Indian Start-up Icons:

- **Embrace Authenticity**: Communicate authentically and honestly. People identify with genuineness and are inclined more to trust and support those who are true to themselves.
- **Master Storytelling**: Use stories to express your vision and values and to create impact. Stories have the ability to engage, inspire, and evoke emotions, making them a powerful communication tool.
- **Listen More, Speak Less:** Practice active listening to understand the needs, concerns, and goals of your team, customers, and stakeholders. Listening increases empathy and trust and fosters relationships.
- **Adapt to Your Audience**: Tailor your communication style to your audience's preferences and expectations. Understanding the perspectives of investors, consumers, and employees and their preferences is critical for successful communication.
- **Transparency and Honesty Build Trust**: Communicate openly and honestly, especially when dealing with difficult situations or expressing disappointing facts. Transparency increases credibility and promotes an environment of confidence and accountability.
- **Seek Feedback**: Communication is a two-way street. Seek feedback from your team, customers, and mentors, and utilise it to create and improve your communication strategy over time, and keep repeating this process.
- **Stay Calm Under Pressure**: Start-up life can be difficult because of ups and downs. Stay calm under pressure

and communicate clearly and effectively, especially in challenging circumstances.

- **Build Relationships**: Communication is more than merely delivering messages. It is also about building relationships. Spend time and effort in establishing connections with your employees, clients, investors, and other stakeholders.
- **Never Stop Learning:** Communication is a skill that can be developed and improved with time. Commit to lifelong learning, be open to possibilities and opportunities for improving your communication skills, and stay current on constantly evolving advancements and best practices in the field of communication.

Key Takeaways

Effective communication is critical in the frequently changing environment of start-ups. By delving into the particular communication issues that start-up founders face while gaining knowledge from the biggest names in the Indian business world, such as Vijay Shekhar Sharma and Shradha Sharma, we can gain valuable insights and practical advice for navigating the communication maze and launching successful businesses.

As we embark on this exciting adventure, let us see communication as an opportunity to inspire, connect, and transform the Indian start-up ecosystem and beyond.

4

Stories of Success

Here, we will look at the experiences of outstanding Indian entrepreneurs who attribute their success to effective communication. We'll learn the value of communication skills on their paths to success through informative case studies and engaging interviews.

Bhavish Aggarwal: Driving Innovation Through Communication

Bhavish Aggarwal, the co-founder of Ola, has been a pivotal figure in transforming India's transportation landscape and expanding his ventures globally. His journey is a compelling case study on how effective communication can foster innovation and growth in the technology industry.

Visionary Leadership and Communication: Bhavish Aggarwal co-founded Ola in 2010 with a clear vision to revolutionise transportation in India. His ability to articulate this vision effectively was crucial in rallying a team around his ideas and driving the company forward. Bhavish's leadership style emphasises transparency and open dialogue, which has been instrumental in building trust and fostering a collaborative environment.

Innovation and Growth: Under Bhavish's leadership, Ola introduced several innovative solutions, including Ola Electric and OlaKrutrim, an Artificial Intelligence (AI) company. These ventures highlight his commitment to leveraging technology for societal benefits and open innovation. Bhavish's emphasis on open standards and protocols contrasts with the American capitalistic approach, positioning India as a leader in open innovation.

Challenges and Resilience: Throughout his career, Bhavish faced numerous challenges, from regulatory hurdles to market competition. His transparent and honest communication helped build trust within his team and with stakeholders, enabling Ola to navigate these challenges successfully. Bhavish's resilience and ability to maintain open lines of communication have been critical to overcoming obstacles and driving continuous growth. In a recent interview, Bhavish shared insights on how communication has been a driving force behind his success. He emphasised the importance of open standards and protocols in technology, advocating for a societal approach to innovation.

Bhavish's ability to communicate these ideas effectively has not only positioned India as a leader in open innovation but also inspired a new generation of entrepreneurs.

Key Takeaways:

- **Clarity of Vision**: Successful entrepreneurs communicate their vision in a straightforward manner, encouraging people to follow them on their path.
- **Persuasive Communication:** Effective communication skills enable entrepreneurs to persuade investors, partners, and customers, contributing to growth and success.
- **Building Relationships:** Entrepreneurs with tremendous communication skills can establish strong relationships with stakeholders, boosting collaboration and trust.
- **Adaptability**: Successful entrepreneurs individualise their communication style to different circumstances and audiences, boosting effect and influence.
- **Continuous Improvement:** Communication skills are not static; they require constant refinement and practice to stay relevant and effective in an ever-changing landscape.

The stories of Vijay Shekhar Sharma, and Bhavish Aggarwal serve as important reminders of how excellent communication may revolutionise businesses. Aspiring entrepreneurs may discover new opportunities and chart their own way to success by learning from their experiences and using their ideas.

- **Mastering Communication**: In the rapidly changing world of start-ups, effective communication is an approach required for survival. In the frequently unforeseen surroundings of entrepreneurship, leaders' ability to communicate clearly, emphatically, and convincingly can mean the difference between success and failure.

Practical techniques for start-up leaders

Section 1: Communication among Team Members

- ***Setting Clear Expectations***: Start off by identifying clearly defined goals, roles, and responsibilities for each team member. Communicate expectations openly and transparently to minimise confusion and encourage responsibility.
- ***Encourage open dialogue*** by creating a culture in which team members feel comfortable sharing their ideas, concerns, and feedback. Actively listen to their points of view while exhibiting compassion and empathy.
- ***Providing Regular Updates:*** Inform team members about the company's growth and development, challenges, and success stories. Regular updates encourage transparency and alignment, which makes everyone motivated and engaged.
- ***Honouring and acknowledging individual and team accomplishments*** might boost morale and build a sense of accomplishment. Recognise contributions and express gratitude for their hard work and dedication.
- ***Addressing Conflicts Promptly***: Resolve team conflicts along with worries in an appropriate and constructive manner. Encourage open communication, make an effort to fully understand every single point of view, and collaborate to develop mutually beneficial solutions.

Section 2: Communicating with Investors

- **Crafting Appealing Pitches**: Create concise and compelling pitches that effectively express your start-up's value proposition, market opportunity, and growth potential. Personalise your message to appeal to the interests and objectives set by potential investors.

- **Establish trust and confidence** with investors by demonstrating integrity, professionalism, and a track record of successful execution. Explain your start-up's obstacles and hazards, as well as how you intend to address them.
- **Providing Regular Updates**: Keep investors informed about major developments, milestones, and performance measures. Provide regular and transparent updates on both accomplishments and setbacks, demonstrating accountability and commitment to the investment.
- **Setting realistic targets and schedules** for growth and return on investment will help manage investors' expectations. Openly discuss prospective obstacles and uncertainties, as well as your plan for dealing with them.
- **Seeking Feedback and Guidance**: Consult with investors about strategic decisions, market trends, and growth possibilities. Use their knowledge and networks to overcome challenges and boost your start-up's growth.

Section 3: Engaging with Stakeholders

- ***Understanding Stakeholder Needs***: Determine and understand the needs, priorities, and concerns of your stakeholders, which include consumers, partners, regulators, and the community. Tailor your communication techniques to their individual interests and goals.
- ***Building Relationships***: Spend time and effort in developing solid relationships with stakeholders based

on trust, transparency, and mutual respect. Engage in two-way interaction, actively listen to their criticism, and demonstrate your sincere commitment to their benefit.

- ***Communicate Impact***: Make it clear how your start-up's products or services will affect stakeholders' lives, businesses, or communities. Emphasise genuine advantages as well as accomplishments and success stories to demonstrate value and find people who support it.
- ***Managing Crisis Communications:*** Plan for and manage future crises or controversies by creating a crisis communication plan. Provide defined standards for reaction and escalation, and communicate openly and transparently with stakeholders to address concerns and mitigate reputational damage.
- ***Sustaining Engagement***: Continue to communicate with stakeholders through regular channels such as newsletters, social media, events, and community outreach programs. Keep them updated, involved, and invested in your start-up's progress and effect.

In the dynamic and competitive start-up environment, good communication is not just a skill; it's a strategic imperative. By managing communication with team members, investors, and stakeholders, start-up CEOs can inspire cooperation, improve coordination, and realise their enterprises' full potential.

As we embark on this new journey together, remember Steve Jobs' words: "Great things in business are never accomplished by one person. They are completed by a team of individuals." Let us leverage the power of good communication to motivate, unite, and propel our start-ups to success.

Top 3 Frustrations:

- **Difficulty in conveying vision to the team**: A lot of start-up owners have trouble articulating their vision and objectives to their team, which causes miscommunication and misunderstandings.
- **Misunderstandings during client negotiations**: Ineffective communication can lead to miscommunications during client negotiations, which can damage agreements and personal connections.
- **Ineffective internal communication**: Delays, mistakes, and lower production can result from ineffective team communication.

Top 3 Fears:

- **Fear of miscommunication resulting in failure**: New businesses are afraid that a misunderstanding could cause serious mistakes or the project or firm to fail.
- **Fear of losing clients because of poor communication**: People worry that having poor communication skills may cause them to lose clients, either current or new.
- **Fear of team conflicts and low morale**: Poor communication can give rise to disputes within the team, which lowers morale and hinders production.

Top 3 Ways to Overcome:

- **Have frequent team meetings to ensure alignment of vision**: Team meetings on a regular basis guarantee that everyone is aware of the objectives and the vision of the organisation.

- **Engage in active listening and empathy exercises**: To better understand clients' requirements and prevent miscommunications, engage in active listening and empathy exercises during interactions with clients.
- **Establishing transparent and open channels of communication**: This is essential for fostering trust and collaboration within a team. To achieve this, it's important to use tools that promote openness, such as shared platforms (e.g., Slack, Microsoft Teams, or Trello), where all team members can access important information, updates, and feedback in real-time.

These tools ensure that everyone is on the same page and that no one feels left out of crucial conversations. Additionally, setting explicit communication protocols—such as defining how often updates should be shared, what kind of information needs to be communicated, and which platforms to use for specific types of communication—helps create clarity and avoids confusion. This structure makes it easier for teams to collaborate, stay informed, and work together toward common goals, all while minimising misunderstandings. Clear, open communication ultimately leads to a more cohesive and efficient work environment.

5

Communication Strategies for Corporate Leaders

Successful leaders should be able to communicate with clarity, empathy, and impact, regardless of whether they are inspiring teams or driving corporate transformation.

In this chapter, we delve into the complexities of corporate communication while focusing on real-life examples such as Sudha Murthy's incredible journey.

Sudha Murthy, a pioneering figure in Indian corporate life, shows the transforming impact of good communication. Murthy led the Infosys Foundation as the chairperson and also established herself as a respected author and philanthropist—her exceptional communication skills mark her leadership journey.

Murthy's communication style has been defined by simplicity, genuineness, and empathy. Whenever she's addressing her Infosys team or dealing with neighbourhood stakeholders, she speaks with a genuine warmth and sincerity that is acknowledged by others. She communicates with people on a human level through her humorous stories and personal experiences, inspiring them to embrace empathy, compassion, and integrity in all their activities.

Sudha Murthy's Insights into Corporate Leader Communication Strategies

- **Lead by Example**: Set an example for the communication skills you want your team to possess. Sudha Murthy's humility and approachability set the tone for open and honest communication at Infosys.
- **Listen Actively**: Prioritise active listening to understand your team members' needs and perspectives. Sudha Murthy's genuine interest in hearing other people's stories promotes inclusivity and collaboration.
- **Communicate with Clarity:** Explain your vision and goals clearly and concisely. Sudha Murthy's effortless communication style ensures that everyone understands the organisation's goals and their respective roles in accomplishing them.
- **Encourage Others**: Empower and encourage your team members to be open about their ideas and opinions. Sudha Murthy's inclusive leadership style emphasises the value of diverse ideas and innovation.
- **Be Authentic**: Communicate authentically and transparently, even in hard situations. Sudha Murthy's honesty and integrity fosters trust and confidence, even during times of crisis.

- **Inspire with Stories**: Use storytelling to convey your message and motivate action. Sudha Murthy's ability to weave fascinating narratives captures listeners and inspires them to make a difference.
- **Adapt to Your Audience**: Customise your communication style to match your audience's tastes and cultural nuances. Sudha Murthy's ability to interact with people of all backgrounds demonstrates her cultural sensitivity and adaptability.
- **Provide Constructive Feedback**: Provide constructive and supportive feedback to help others grow and develop. Sudha Murthy's mentorship and advice enable people to attain their best potential.
- **Boost Morale with Recognition:** Recognising and celebrating accomplishments can enhance morale and reinforce favcurable behaviours. Sudha Murthy's humility and respect for other people's contributions foster a culture of gratitude and collaboration.
- **Continuous Improvement**: Adopt a growth mentality and actively seek opportunities to improve your communication skills. Sudha Murthy's lifetime dedication to learning and self-improvement motivates others to pursue excellence.

Sudha Murthy's leadership journey provides invaluable lessons about the communication tactics corporate executives should learn. Effective communication can be seen as a mind-set—a commitment to facilitating understanding, collaboration, and development within and beyond organisations.

As business leaders, let us embrace communication's transforming ability to inspire, empower, and lead with purpose and passion. As Sudha Murthy put it, "Great leaders are not defined by their titles or positions; they are defined by their ability to communicate, inspire, and bring out the best in others." Let us rise to the challenge of unleashing our leadership's full potential through effective communication.

Mastering Leadership Through Effective Communication

Communication skills are a lot more than additional commodities in the rapidly changing environment of corporate leadership, they are an essential component of effective leadership. Being capable to communicate clearly, effectively and empathetically is necessary for inspiring teams, managing problems, promoting innovation, and driving development.

Let us understand the complicated structure of communication in corporate leadership, examining its role, influence, and significance in the Indian setting.

The Foundation of Leadership

Every successful organisation requires an inspirational leader who can explain an inspiring purpose, align different stakeholders, and encourage collective action.

Communication is the foundation upon which this leadership can be built, enabling leaders to communicate their ideas with clarity, conviction, and transparency.

In the Indian business landscape, where an array of cultures, languages, and perspectives abound, effective communication becomes even more crucial for developing unity, trust, and collaboration.

Navigating Challenges with Communication

In the fast-paced environment of the business world, challenges are unavoidable, ranging from market disruptions to organisational conflicts. When confronted with hardship, the actual capability of leadership communication shines through. Leaders who can communicate openly, empathetically, and strongly are better positioned to negotiate crises, manage change, and rally their teams toward a shared vision, ensuring resilience and success in the face of adversity.

Through effective communication, leaders can instil confidence, foster resilience, and transform challenges into opportunities for growth and innovation.

Developing a Culture of Engagement

In today's knowledge-driven economy, organisations thrive on the intelligence and creativity of their employees. Developing a culture of engagement is crucial for fostering an environment where team members feel valued, heard, and empowered to reach their full potential.

Effective leadership communication is at the heart of this engagement. Leaders must cultivate open lines of communication, encouraging employees to share their ideas and feedback. This not only enhances collaboration but also creates a sense of belonging and ownership among team members.

Driving Performance and Results

Leadership effectiveness is measured by its ability to create actual outcomes and drive long-term growth. Communication skills are essential in this area, allowing leaders to establish clear expectations, provide constructive feedback, and encourage high-performing teams. Communicating effectively allows leaders to coordinate with their teams around common goals, evaluate progress, and celebrate accomplishments.

To conclude, effective communication is the key to leadership excellence, from establishing a compelling vision to managing hurdles, encouraging engagement, and driving performance.

Let us, as leaders in the Indian business landscape, embrace communication's ground-breaking power, identifying it as an essential component of leadership success rather than a mere skill. Let us use our words, actions, and connections to inspire, empower, and lead with purpose, integrity, and impact.

Masters of Communication: Leading Today's Corporates

Let's look at the stories of widely recognised business leaders who have mastered the art of communication, motivating individuals, driving innovation, and redefining India's commercial landscape.

1. **Ratan Tata**: The former Chairman of Tata Sons was renowned for his humility, vision, and clarity of communication. He demonstrated leadership via effective communication. From his motivational speeches to his frank interviews, Tata's ability to define his vision for the Tata Group and involve stakeholders at all levels garnered him worldwide appreciation and respect.
2. **Aditya Puri**: The former CEO of HDFC Bank is well-known for his effortless communication style and enduring dedication towards client satisfaction. Puri's ability to communicate complicated financial ideas in simple terms, as well as his honest interactions with employees and shareholders, have helped HDFC Bank accomplish

success while maintaining its reputation as one of India's premier banks.

3. **Nirmala Sitharaman**: India's first female Finance Minister has made an effect not only through her policy decisions but also through her strong communication skills. Sitharaman's straightforward yet confident delivery at budget presentations and press conferences has garnered her praise for her ability to engage and inform the public about crucial economic concerns.
4. **Mukesh Ambani**: Chairman and Managing Director of Reliance Industries Limited, has been recognised for his creative management and persuasive ability to communicate. Ambani's annual shareholder meetings, during which he discusses Reliance's big ambitions for development and innovation, are strongly regarded and appreciated for their clarity, optimism, and strategic vision.
5. **Kiran Mazumdar-Shaw:** The Founder and Chairperson of Biocon Limited, Kiran Mazumdar-Shaw, is a pioneer in the biotechnology business with remarkable communication abilities. Mazumdar-Shaw's ability to articulate complicated scientific concepts in an understandable manner, as well as her enthusiasm for innovation and entrepreneurship, has earned her recognition in both the business and scientific worlds.
6. **Anand Mahindra:** The Chairman of the Mahindra Group, is known for his engaging and inclusive communication approach. Mahindra's active participation on social media sites, where he offers insights, interacts with followers, and

responds to customer questions, illustrates his dedication to transparency, accessibility, and customer engagement.

7. **Shikha Sharma**: Former CEO of Axis Bank, Sharma was recognised for her strategic vision and communication skills. Under Sharma's leadership, Axis Bank rose to the position of one of India's leading private sector banks by successfully conveying the bank's growth plan, addressing problems, and engaging stakeholders.
8. **Uday Kotak:** Kotak Mahindra Bank's Managing Director and CEO is respected for his excellent leadership and communication skills. Kotak's clear vision, strong communication style, and concentration on ethical banking have garnered him respect among peers, workers, and investors alike.
9. **Kumar Mangalam Birla:** Aditya Birla Group's Kumar Mangalam Birla has successfully communicated his vision for the Aditya Birla Group through a narrative that emphasises sustainability and social responsibility.

   He has championed the idea of 'Responsibility' as a core value and communicated this consistently across all platforms, from investor meetings to public forums. His storytelling ability has inspired not just employees but also consumers, positioning the brand as a leader in corporate social responsibility.

In today's dynamic corporate environment, effective communication transcends mere information sharing; it serves as a driving force for inspiration, collaboration, and transformation.

The tales of these well-known corporate executives demonstrate the importance of communication in achieving success, building trust, and defining a brighter future for India's corporate environment.

As we are inspired by these examples, let us seek to grow and improve our own communication abilities, acknowledging their enormous potential to lead, influence, and impact the world.

In today's dynamic corporate landscape, effective communication is far more than a skill; it is the bedrock of outstanding leadership. Business leaders who have mastered the art of communication not only excel in motivating individuals and driving innovation but also redefine the commercial landscape.

For instance, leaders like Falguni Nayar of Nykaa have demonstrated how exceptional communication can transform industries. By clearly articulating their vision, engaging with stakeholders, and fostering a culture of openness, these leaders inspire their teams, influence customer perceptions, and propel their companies to new heights.

Effective communication has played a crucial role in the growth and success of leading business figures. By mastering both verbal and non-verbal communication, leaders can effectively convey their ideas, build strong relationships, and navigate complex situations.

Nayar's ability to communicate Nykaa's mission and values clearly helped establish the brand as a leader in the beauty and wellness sector. Her strategic use of communication channels ensured that Nykaa's message reached and resonated with a wide audience, driving significant business growth and customer loyalty.

How Communication Skills Benefit Everyday Life

Building Stronger Relationships: Effective communication helps in establishing and maintaining strong personal and professional relationships. By listening actively and expressing oneself clearly, individuals can foster trust, resolve conflicts, and connect with others on a deeper level.

Enhancing Professional Opportunities: In the workplace, strong communication skills can open doors to career advancement and new opportunities. Being able to articulate ideas, collaborate effectively, and present oneself confidently can lead to greater visibility and career growth.

> "The art of communication is the language of leadership."
>
> —James Humes

Communication Expertise: Lessons from India's Icons

Every relationship, whether personal or professional, depends upon effective communication.

In this part of the chapter, we'll investigate the art of communication through the viewpoints of real-life Indian celebrities who have mastered the ability to deal with challenging conversations, deliver successful presentations, and establish communicative corporate cultures.

Handling Difficult Conversations: Deepika Padukone's Perspective

Deepika Padukone, a well-known Bollywood actress and mental health advocate, displays elegance under pressure when it comes to dealing with challenging topics.

Padukone has held numerous conversations with individuals, families, and legislators in her attempt to reduce the stigma associated with mental health concerns, exposing taboos and generating change.

Key Insights:

- She handles tough situations with empathy, attempting to understand people's points of view and perspectives.
- Padukone's openness and vulnerability create a safe space for people to speak out and express their own mental health difficulties.
- She actively listens without judgment, allowing people to fully express themselves and feel heard.
- She takes a solution-oriented approach, focusing on identifying answers and providing support while steering conversations toward positive outcomes.

N. R. Narayana Murthy, co-founder of Infosys, is renowned for his ability to deliver clear and impactful presentations.

Here are some key insights from his approach:

- **Simplicity and Clarity:** Murthy emphasises the importance of keeping messages simple and clear. He believes that a presentation should be easily understandable by everyone in the audience, regardless of their background.
- **Thorough Preparation:** He spends significant time preparing his presentations to ensure they are well-structured and informative. This includes rehearsing multiple times to refine the delivery.
- **Storytelling:** Using stories and real-life examples to illustrate points makes the presentation more engaging and relatable. Murthy often shares anecdotes from his own experiences to connect with the audience.
- **Effective Use of Visual Aids:** Visual aids are used to support the message and keep the audience engaged. Murthy

ensures that his slides are not cluttered and that each visual element adds value to the presentation.

Priyanka Chopra: A global icon and successful actress, she has mastered the art of communication, particularly in delivering impactful presentations.

Here are some key insights from her approach:

- **Confidence and Presence:** Chopra exudes confidence and maintains a strong presence on stage. She believes that confidence is key to engaging the audience and delivering a memorable presentation.
- **Clear Articulation**: She emphasises the importance of clear and articulate speech. This ensures that the audience can easily understand and follow the message being conveyed.
- **Storytelling:** Like many effective communicators, Chopra uses storytelling to make her presentations more engaging. She often shares personal anecdotes and experiences to connect with her audience on a deeper level.
- **Passion and Enthusiasm:** Speaking with passion and enthusiasm is another hallmark of Chopra's presentation style. Her energy and enthusiasm are infectious, helping to keep the audience engaged and interested throughout the presentation.

As we attempt to replicate the communication abilities of these Indian legends, keep in mind that communication is more than merely words—it is about connection, understanding, and empowerment. Let us use the power of communication to establish bridges, inspire change, and create a better future for everyone.

Top 3 Frustrations

- **Miscommunication**: Miscommunication among team members causes errors, delays, and lost production, which frequently irritates corporate bosses. This can lead to arguments, erode team spirit, and produce a demanding work atmosphere.
- **Absence of Interest in Meetings**: In meetings, leaders often have to deal with disengaged team members, which makes it difficult to get essential messages across and accomplish desired results. This may lead to ineffective decision-making, a lack of agreement on objectives, and time wastage.
- **Unreliable Messaging**: It can be a challenge to maintain uniform communication at all organisational levels, particularly when signals are misinterpreted during transmission. This leads to a loss of trust between management and staff, as well as confusion and misaligned goals.

Top 3 Fears

- **Fear of Public Speaking:** Speaking in front of a big group of people, taking part in important meetings, or interacting with the media can all cause anxiety for business executives. Their capacity to motivate and lead their teams or to properly represent their organisation may be hampered by this anxiety.
- **Fear of Not Being Understood:** Managers worry that their staff won't fully comprehend what they're saying, which

could lead to poorly carried-out plans and projects. As a result, the organisation may experience a loss of direction, a decline in efficiency, and missed opportunities.

- **Fear of Conflict:** Corporate leaders frequently fear having to handle disagreements or provide unfavourable comments. They fear hurting people's feelings or coming off poorly. Ignoring conflict can lead to unsolved problems, smouldering animosity, and a hostile work atmosphere.

Top 3 Ways to Overcome Communication Challenges

- **Invest in Communication Training:** Engage in comprehensive communication skills training to enhance your ability to communicate messages clearly and confidently. This can reduce miscommunication, improve public speaking abilities, and boost overall effectiveness in leadership roles.
- **Implement Active Listening Practices:** Practice active listening, which involves fully concentrating, understanding, responding, and remembering what is being said. Active listening can improve engagement in meetings, ensure consistent messaging, and build stronger relationships with team members.
- **Promote a Feedback Culture:** Foster a culture where giving and receiving constructive feedback is normalised and encouraged. Provide tools and frameworks for effective feedback. This can help overcome the fear of conflict, address issues promptly, and create a transparent and trustful work environment.

6

Communicating Like a Champion: Lessons from Indian Sports Icons

Effective communication in sports is about more than just transmitting messages; it's also about inspiring, motivating, and coordinating successes. Let's find out how some of India's most prominent sportsmen learned communication skills.

Also, look more closely at the role of communication in sports performance and team chemistry, using real-life examples from Indian sports figures.

Leading by Example: Sachin Tendulkar, also known as the 'God of Cricket,' shows the power of leading by example. Tendulkar's on-field communication was more than just words; it was also about actions. His drive, work ethic, and unwavering pursuit of excellence inspired his teammates to mirror his commitment and passion. Tendulkar's ability to communicate through performance not only enhanced his own game but also had a significant impact on team morale and dynamics.

Positive Reinforcement: PV Sindhu, India's badminton star and Olympic silver winner, acknowledges the need of positive reinforcement in communication. Sindhu's interactions with her coaches and teammates have been identified by expressions of encouragement, support, and belief. Sindhu not only enhances her own confidence by communicating positively, but she also lifts the spirits of those around her. Positive reinforcement is important for improving collaboration among teammates and their performance because it makes athletes feel valued and encouraged to give their all.

Emotional Intelligence: Sachin Tendulkar, revered as the "Master Blaster," exemplifies how emotional intelligence can enhance communication skills.

His ability to listen actively, whether to coaches, teammates, or during press interactions, demonstrates his attentiveness and respect for others' perspectives.

Tendulkar's calm demeanour under pressure showcases his emotional regulation, allowing him to maintain focus and deliver consistent performances.

Clear Communication: Mary Kom, India's boxing superstar and Olympic bronze winner, emphasises on the need for open communication in sports. As a coach and mentor for prospective athletes, Mary Kom emphasises on the significance of properly communicating goals, methods, and expectations. Her straightforward communication style eliminates ambiguity and ensures that athletes properly understand their roles and duties.

These real-life examples exemplify how excellent communication is not just an instrument for communicating information but also a catalyst for athletic success.

Cristiano Ronaldo's communication skills have played a crucial role in his success both on and off the field.

Practical tips inspired by his approach:

- **Learn Multiple Languages:** Ronaldo is fluent in Portuguese, English, Spanish, and Italian, which helps him connect with diverse teammates and fans.
- **Practice Regularly:** He continuously works on his language skills, even hiring private tutors to improve his proficiency.
- **Be Confident:** Ronaldo's confidence in expressing himself, whether in interviews or team meetings, enhances his leadership presence.
- **Use Positive Reinforcement:** He often encourages and motivates his teammates, fostering a positive team environment.
- **Lead by Example:** Ronaldo's dedication and work ethic set a standard for others to follow.
- **Show Emotional Intelligence:** He is known for his ability to manage emotions and stay composed under pressure.
- **Engage with Fans:** Ronaldo actively communicates with his fans through social media, maintaining a strong connection with his global audience.
- **Adapt to New Environments**: His ability to quickly adapt to new teams and cultures showcases his flexible communication style.
- **Be Clear and Concise:** Ronaldo ensures his messages are straightforward and easily understood, avoiding misunderstandings.

- **Seek Feedback:** He values feedback from coaches and teammates to continuously improve his communication and performance.

Individuals and teams can improve performance, strengthen team chemistry, and achieve goals on and off the pitch by taking notice of what he does and putting his advice into practice.

In sports, coaches play a much more important role than merely being technically proficient. They also need to be leaders, motivators, and good communicators. Pullela Gopichand, the renowned badminton coach who has trained some of India's best players, including Olympic medalists Saina Nehwal and PV Sindhu, is a model figure in this field.

The foundation of Gopichand's coaching philosophy is developing close personal bonds with each of his players. He highlighted the need for empathy and mindful listening, as these are crucial for comprehending the unique needs and motivations of each athlete.

Gopichand not only teaches technical skills but also instils confidence and self-belief in players—two qualities that are essential for success on and off the court—by fostering an atmosphere in which players feel free to express themselves.

Another legend in Indian sports coaching is Ravi Shastri, a former cricket player who became a coach and made an eternal impact on the sport. Shastri, who is well-known for his charismatic attitude and elegant communication skills, shares insightful information about his teaching philosophy in his interviews. The idea of candid and open communication is fundamental to his methodology.

The success of the Indian cricket team has been greatly attributed to Shastri's capacity for developing personal connections with players and his gift for giving inspirational speeches.

Shastri stresses the significance of developing a supportive team environment based on mutual respect and trust, where all players, regardless of experience or background, feel appreciated and heard.

Harendra Singh is a shining example of leadership and inspiration in the hockey world. Singh is a coach who wears his love for the game on his sleeve. His interviews provide insight into his contagious energy and steadfast dedication to perfection.

By means of lucid and efficient communication, Singh enables his players to rise to the occasion and pursue excellence. India's success in the international arena has been greatly attributed to his capacity to communicate intricate tactical concepts in a way that his players can understand.

Singh's interviews underscore the significance of establishing a loving and encouraging atmosphere that inspires players to perform to the best of their abilities, not only for their own benefit but also for the team's overall success.

Lessons on teamwork, motivation, and resilience can be gleaned from the world of sports. Surpassing the confines of the playing field, these insights reveal priceless perspectives relevant to a multitude of different dimensions of existence.

Top 3 Frustrations

- **Misinterpretation of Intentions and Messages**: Sports icons often feel pressurised and frustrated when their statements or actions are misinterpreted by the media or the public, leading to unwanted controversies and misunderstandings.

- **Inability to Articulate Emotions Under Pressure:** During certain moments, athletes may struggle to express their thoughts and emotions clearly, affecting their interactions with teammates, coaches, and the media.
- **Language Barriers**: For athletes who primarily speak regional languages, communicating effectively in English or Hindi (for broader media coverage) can be a significant challenge, leading to frustration and loss of confidence.

Top 3 Fears

- **Fear of Public Speaking:** Many sports icons fear speaking in front of large audiences or the media, worrying about making mistakes or being judged by the public.
- **Fear of Negative Media Coverage:** The fear that any miscommunication or slip of the tongue could be blown out of proportion by the media, affecting one's public image and career.
- **Fear of Cultural Misunderstandings:** Concerns about unintentionally offending others due to cultural differences or lack of understanding, especially in international contexts or multicultural team environments.

Top 3 Ways to Overcome

- **Professional Training and Workshops:** Engage in regular communication skills training and public speaking workshops. Learning from experts can help sports personalities develop confidence and clarity in their communication.
- **Media Coaching:** Hire media coaches to prepare for interviews and public appearances. Media coaching can

help athletes learn how to handle tough questions, stay focused on their message, and project a positive image.

- **Practice and Feedback:** Practice speaking in different settings, such as team meetings, press conferences, and public events. Seek feedback from trusted mentors or communication specialists to continually improve and refine your skills.

7

The Celebrity Communicator: Navigating Public Image

Navigating public images is essential for Indian celebrities, as it involves balancing their personal lives with their public personas to maintain a positive and relatable image.

For example, Shah Rukh Khan skillfully uses social media to connect with fans by sharing personal moments and engaging in conversations while maintaining his status as the "King of Bollywood."

The Power of Perception

Public Relations and Celebrity Branding: Public Relations (PR) for celebrities involves managing their public image and reputation through strategic communication and media relations. PR professionals craft compelling narratives, handle media inquiries, and manage social media presence to ensure positive visibility and engagement.

Celebrity Branding focuses on creating a strong, consistent personal brand that resonates with the audience. This includes securing endorsements, partnerships, and public appearances that align with the celebrity's image and values.

Effective branding helps celebrities maintain relevance and appeal in the public eye.

Reputation management strategies and celebrity branding strategies are built on the foundation of effective communication, which is essential for creating and sustaining these visions.

In this chapter, we will explore the methods and approaches used by celebrity communicators to negotiate the frequently changing terrain of the media industry, exploring the complex relationship between communication and public image management.

Identifying the Celebrity Persona: Every effective celebrity brand is built around an individual with whom audiences connect. To define and uphold this identity consistently across multiple platforms of media and public appearances, effective communication is important.

Every communication, from red-carpet interviews to social media posts, adds to the story around the celebrity, so it's critical for their communication team to match every message with audience expectations and brand values.

Strategic Media Engagement: Celebrities need to negotiate a media world full of potential risks in the era of endless news cycles and viral content. Proficient communicators understand the significance of deliberately engaging with the media, leveraging interviews, press releases, and media appearances to favourably mould the story around their clients. Effective communication techniques help celebrities manage their public image and stay relevant in the public eye, whether they are handling controversies or promoting new ventures.

Building Real Connections: Good communication continues to rely heavily on authenticity, even while retaining a polished public image is important. By highlighting genuine interactions and heartfelt moments, communicators can enhance a celebrity's brand and public image, fostering deeper fan loyalty and trust. This approach not only humanises the celebrity but also strengthens the emotional bond with their audience, ensuring long-term engagement and support.

Crisis Management: Emergencies are bound to occur in the unpredictable world of celebrities. Having competent crisis management abilities is essential for preserving a positive public image in the face of scandals and bad news.

In times of crisis, good communication helps protect the integrity of the celebrity brand and minimise the damage to one's reputation. Celebrity communicators are essential in handling difficult situations and regaining the public's faith, whether they are apologising, performing damage control interviews, or directly addressing issues on social media.

Using Social Media: As social media platforms have grown in popularity as well, superstars now have never-before-seen access to their fanbase, but they also come with more scrutiny and possible negative feedback.

Competent communicators are aware of the complexities of social media communication, making use of sites like Instagram,

Twitter, and TikTok to establish genuine connections with followers while staying clear of misunderstandings that can harm their brand.

Effective social media communication is crucial to a celebrity's digital footprint and building a devoted online following from creating captivating material to replying to fan feedback.

Working with Brand Partners: In today's celebrity-driven market, brand collaborations offer a profitable way for celebrities to increase their visibility and impact.

The alignment of values, communications, and objectives depends on the celebrity, the management team, and the brand partners' effective communication.

In order to improve a celebrity's public image and marketability through brand relationships, celebrity communicators are essential in everything from negotiating endorsement deals to co-creating marketing campaigns.

Measuring Impact and Success: In the quick-paced professions of public relations and celebrity branding, evaluating the effect of communication strategies is essential to determining their effectiveness and providing recommendations for future moves.

Communicators use a wide range of methods and techniques to measure the success of their efforts, from analysing social media engagement metrics to conducting audience polls.

Through the investigation of data and feedback, they can enhance their plans to more effectively connect with audiences and accomplish the intended results for their customers.

In summary, the secret to successful celebrity branding and public relations is excellent communication. Competent communicators are essential for maintaining public image and building real relationships with audiences, from constructing the celebrity persona to handling crises and utilising social media.

Celebrities may build a devoted fan following, stay relevant in the rapidly evolving media landscape, and increase their marketability in the cutthroat entertainment sector by utilising smart communication techniques.

Examining case studies of Indian celebrities who have successfully used communication to manage their public image offers important insights into the methods and techniques they use to keep a favourable image in the face of public and media scrutiny.

We'll look at a few prominent cases in this, analysing their communication strategies, difficulties they encountered, and the results of their work.

- **Deepika Padukone**: One of Bollywood's top actresses, she has demonstrated a deep awareness of how much impact communication has on the general public. She not only transformed herself by sharing her experiences with depression, but she also started a national dialogue on mental health. She successfully transformed a personal struggle into a platform for societal change through her advocacy work and open interviews, winning widespread recognition and respect in the process.
- **Shah Rukh Khan**: Often referred to as the "King of Bollywood," Khan is well-known for his charm and personality off-screen in addition to his on-screen impact. He has kept up a largely favourable public image with his humorous remarks, respectful demeanour, and charitable endeavours—despite the odd controversy. Khan has established a devoted fan base that straddles generations and

geographic borders by utilising his enormous popularity and interacting with fans on social media, solidifying his place as one of India's most adored celebrities.

- **Priyanka Chopra Jonas**: Through a mix of talent, drive, and smart communication, Priyanka Chopra Jonas, a former Miss World who is now an actress and global star, has effectively controlled her public image. She has constantly maintained her public profile while carefully designing her image to appeal to a wide range of viewers worldwide, whether it is through her pioneering achievements in Hollywood, her vocal support of gender equality, or her high-profile marriage to musician Nick Jonas.
- **Kangana Ranaut**: Ranaut has constantly courted controversy due to her fiery attitude and outspoken temperament. But she's also acquired an enthusiastic following and a lot of media attention for her unapologetic openness and courage to speak her views. She has drawn criticism from certain places, but she has endured in her beliefs and has garnered exposure for herself through her films, interviews, and social media posts, proving the value of remaining true to oneself in the face of difficulty.
- **Salman Khan**: Through a mix of box office success, humanitarian activity, and a devoted fan base, Khan has managed to maintain his standing as one of Bollywood's top stars despite various legal difficulties and controversies. Even though his reputation has occasionally been damaged, he has managed to come out on top thanks to his ability to engage viewers with his on-screen presence and charitable work.

To sum everything up, the study of Indian celebrities' case studies here focuses on how crucial good communication is for maintaining one's public persona. Celebrities have utilised diverse strategies, such as transparency, advocacy, charisma, or genuineness, to effectively manage the challenges of media scrutiny and stardom.

Ultimately, this has resulted in a favourable public view of them. Aspiring celebrities might aim to imitate their success and establish enduring relationships with their audiences by taking lessons from their experiences and comprehending the fundamentals of good communication.

Here are some tips to maintain authenticity:

- **Know Yourself**: Being genuine requires that you are aware of your values, beliefs, and strengths. Invest some time in introspection to determine your top priorities.
- **Adopt Transparency**: Trust is cultivated via transparency. Be transparent and truthful while sharing information, particularly when addressing problems or difficulties.
- **Stay True to Your Values**: You should act in a way that is consistent with your values. Don't let temporary success force you to sacrifice your morals.
- **Be Sincere**: Being sincere and real is the foundation of authenticity. Don't pretend to be someone you're not or put on a front.
- **Acknowledge Your Mistakes**: Errors happen to everyone. Be transparent about them, accept responsibility, and draw lessons from them. It exudes genuineness and humility.
- **Listen to Feedback**: Pay attention to what people are saying

about you and have an open mind to helpful critiques. Take criticism to heart and develop.

- **Remain Consistent**: Your authenticity is strengthened when you act, speak, and behave consistently. Those who are dependable and consistent are considered trustworthy by the public.
- **Be Vulnerable**: You can build stronger relationships with people by being open about your weaknesses and challenges. It proves you're a relatable human being.
- **Refrain from Overpromising**: Have a reasonable expectation of your abilities. Authenticity and trust are damaged by overpromising and underdelivering.
- **Show Empathy**: Show kindness and sympathy for other people. So that relationships are strengthened and rapport is increased.

Handling Media Interviews: While media interviews can be difficult, they also offer a chance to spread your message to a larger audience. The following advice can help you handle media interviews well.

- **Be Prepared Fully**: Do some advanced research on the issue, the interviewer, and the media outlet. Be aware of your points of reference and important messages.
- **Practice Active Listening**: As you respond to the interviewer's questions, pay careful consideration to what they are addressing. Give yourself some time to gather your thoughts before responding.
- **Remain focused on the message**: Even if the interviewer asks irrelevant questions, keep your attention on delivering

your main points. Relink to your primary points whenever it is feasible.

- **Incorporate Examples and Stories**: To make your points more comprehensible and captivating, use suitable instances or stories to illustrate your points.
- **Embrace Tough Questions**: When faced with a challenging inquiry, accept it, give a succinct answer, and then move the conversation to a more upbeat subject.
- **Address Difficult Questions Gracefully**: When explaining complicated subjects, use language that is simple to understand.
- **Avoid Jargon**: When explaining complicated subjects, use language that is simple to understand.
- **Be Respectful**: Regardless of your disagreement with the interviewer's or the audience's opinions, show them some consideration.
- **Follow-up:** Express gratitude to the interviewer for their time and extend an offer to provide more details if necessary.

Navigating Social Media

Social media offers a powerful platform for connecting with others and sharing your message, but it also presents challenges in terms of maintaining authenticity and managing your online presence. Here are some tips for navigating social media effectively:

- **Identify Your Brand:** Decide on your desired social media persona and tailor your interactions and material to suit.
- **Be Selective:** Pick the social media sites that best fit your objectives and intended audience. Being active and involved in a select handful is preferable to spreading thin over numerous platforms.

- **Engage Authentically:** When interacting on social media, show that you are sincere and real. Steer clear of generic communications and automatic responses.
- **Exchange Useful Content**: Give your audience something that will inspire, educate, or amuse them. Give priority to quality above quantity.
- **Maintain Uniformity**: Maintain visibility and engagement by adhering to a regular posting schedule. Maintaining consistency promotes credibility and confidence.
- **Pay Attention and React**: Keep an eye on discussions about your company or sector and reply to inquiries, comments, and critiques right away.
- **Monitor Your Reputation**: Pay attention to what others are saying on social media about you or your company. Resolve any unfavourable comments or false facts right away.
- **Make Good Use of Visuals**: On social media, visual content—such as photos and videos—performs better. To strengthen your point and grab readers' attention, use images.
- **Be Formal**: Even when sharing personal opinions or having casual conversations on social media, always keep your tone and behaviour professional.
- **Examine Your Privacy Settings**: Make sure you are happy with who may access your posts and information by regularly reviewing your privacy settings.

Whether you're using social media for personal branding or representing an organisation, you can take on media interviews with confidence, stay true to yourself, and follow these strategies to navigate the platform with ease. Always keep in mind that developing genuine relationships and establishing trust both offline and online depend on genuineness.

Authenticity has become essential to a celebrity's capability to develop and maintain a successful public persona in today's hyper-connected community. Authenticity is key, whether you're interacting with fans on social media or addressing the media in interviews. This chapter examines how superstars can maintain their authenticity in the face of media appearances and social media, with real-life examples from Indian celebrities who have perfected the skill.

Authenticity in Media Interviews:

- **Self-Discovery**: It's critical that celebrities have an in-depth understanding of their values, boundaries, and identities before they interact with the media. Authenticity is based on this self-awareness.
- **Maintain Transparency**: Trust should be established between the audience and celebrities. Even if it involves owning up to errors or weaknesses, celebrities should be open and truthful in their responses.
- **Remain True to Your Point of View**: Reliability is essential. Celebrities should make sure that, in every interview, their messaging reflects their brand image and beliefs.
- **Steer Clear of Canned Responses**: Even while preparation is key, answers that are too prepared may come out as fake. Celebrities should instead put their attention towards interacting with people in a sincere and unplanned manner.
- **Listen and Respond:** Active listening is crucial during interviews. Celebrities should pay attention to the

interviewer's questions and respond thoughtfully rather than simply delivering pre-planned responses.

Example: Selena Gomez exemplifies authenticity in media interviews, particularly in how she navigates social media.

Here are four key points:

- **Openly Discussing Mental Health:** Selena candidly shares her struggles with mental health, emphasising the importance of self-care and taking breaks from social media.
- **Delegating Social Media Management:** She has delegated her social media passwords to her team, allowing her to focus on her well-being without the constant pressure of online presence.
- **Promoting Digital Detox:** By deleting social media apps from her phone, Selena advocates for digital detoxes, highlighting the relief and liberation that come from disconnecting.
- **Encouraging Vulnerability:** Her transparency about her personal challenges encourages her audience to embrace vulnerability and prioritise their mental health.

Example: Sunil Chhetri, the iconic Indian footballer, exemplifies authenticity in media interviews through his adept use of communication skills.

Known for his genuine and heartfelt interactions, Chhetri emphasises the importance of balance and mental well-being. He often shares how he manages his online presence without letting it dominate his life.

Chhetri also advocates for using social media as a platform for positive engagement and inspiration rather than a source of stress. He sets clear boundaries, such as limiting screen time and prioritising real-life interactions, to maintain his mental health.

By being transparent about his own experiences and challenges, Chhetri connects deeply with his audience, encouraging them to adopt healthier digital habits.

His approach underscores the value of authenticity, mindfulness, and effective communication in the digital age, making him a relatable and influential figure both on and off the field.

7

Digital Communication

Digital communication has transformed how we interact with one another, research, and perform our jobs in today's highly connected society. It has become an essential part of our life.

The experiences of Indian celebrities may teach us a lot about efficiently utilising the power of digital communication as we make our way through this digital landscape.

While conversations are usually dominated by sports personalities and Bollywood celebrities, there are a lot more well-known individuals whose techniques and online personas can teach us important lessons.

Among these is Elon Musk's communication skills, which provide a compelling example of how digital communication can transform interactions and influence in today's connected society. Musk's use of Twitter is particularly noteworthy.

He leverages the platform to engage directly with his audience, share updates, and even makes major announcements about his companies.

This direct and unfiltered communication style fosters a sense of transparency and approachability, making him relatable to his followers.

Musk's ability to articulate complex ideas in simple terms is another key aspect of his digital communication prowess.

Whether discussing advancements in electric vehicles or space exploration, he breaks down intricate concepts into understandable language, ensuring his messages resonate with a broad audience.

Additionally, his strategic use of pauses and thoughtful responses during interviews enhances the impact of his communication, allowing his audience to absorb and reflect on his messages.

By combining clarity, transparency, and strategic engagement, Musk exemplifies how effective digital communication can build strong connections, influence public perception, and drive brand success in the digital age.

Warren Buffett emphasises the importance of clear and effective communication. He believes that the ability to convey ideas clearly can significantly enhance one's influence and success. Buffett's approach includes using simple, relatable language to explain complex financial concepts, making them accessible to a broader audience. He also values transparency and honesty, often sharing his thoughts and strategies openly in his annual letters to shareholders. This builds trust and credibility, essential components of effective digital communication.

In the realm of sports, legendary tennis star **Mahesh Bhupathi** has also grown significantly in terms of digital media platforms.

Beyond his accomplishments on the court, Bhupathi saw how digital media could be used to promote tennis and interact with fans worldwide.

Bhupathi makes excellent use of social media to answer queries from viewers, provide fans with behind-the-scenes glimpses at events, and share details about his training routine. Bhupathi earned an avid following beyond the world of tennis by transforming his online image and offering genuine insights into his life as a professional player.

The incorporation of Virtual Reality (VR) technology by Bhupathi to give fans a more comprehensive championship experience is an example of his digital engagement. Bhupathi has made use of cutting-edge technology to improve fan contact and promote himself as a modern figure in the sports sector. In order to improve digital communication tactics, Bhupathi's method highlights the significance of embracing innovation and keeping up with new technology.

Renowned author and social critic, **Arundhati Roy** has effectively leveraged online communication as a means of advocacy and social change in the literary and activist realms. Roy has addressed a wide range of important problems, from environmental protection to human rights, through her insightful essays, interviews, and social media presence.

The author has broadened her audience and created significant discussions about problems that are frequently overlooked within popular culture using digital media effectively. Her commitment to digital activism is demonstrated by her effective utilisation of social media platforms that helps grassroots causes and vulnerable individuals. By transforming the voices of opposition or fostering support for environmental concerns, Roy's digital activism has inspired collaboration and support from a wide range of people.

Roy's circumstances demonstrate the revolutionary impact of digital communication in uplifting voices that are underrepresented in society.

In conclusion, an expert understanding of platforms, content, and audience engagement techniques is necessary to effectively navigate digital communication in the present day.

Indian icons such as Mahesh Bhupathi and Arundhati Roy provide us with valuable insights into how we can use digital platforms. These influential people show how digital communication can alter narratives, ignite conversations, and have a beneficial impact on society—whether through authenticity, social change, or meaningful friendships.

Navigating the Digital Landscape

Possibilities and Challenges in Communication: The digital age has resulted in a significant shift in communication, which offers advantages as well as challenges for individuals and communities.

The rise of social media platforms and the widespread use of smartphones have had a major impact on the way we share information with one another. This part of the chapter examines the various aspects of communication in the digital age, looking at both the obstacles that exist and the opportunities that lie ahead.

We explore their knowledge and viewpoints through the eyes of another well-known Indian figure in order to shed light on the complexities of this changing environment.

Raghuram Rajan renowned economist and former governor of the Reserve Bank of India provides an insightful analysis of the opportunities and problems associated with communication in the digital era.

Rajan has highlighted the relationship of finance, technology, and policy throughout his distinguished career, offering insightful thoughts on the effects of digitalisation on the global economy.

Challenges

- **Digital Gap**: Although digital technologies are widely accessible, a significant percentage of the population in India and around the world lacks access to strong internet connectivity. Rajan highlights the importance of addressing the digital gap to guarantee proper participation in the digital economy.
- **Information Overload**: People are overloaded with information due to the rapid expansion of social media and internet content, which makes it difficult to separate fact from fiction. Rajan emphasises the importance of media literacy and critical thinking abilities in navigating this information.
- **Privacy Concerns**: With the increasing digitisation of society, data security and privacy have emerged as the primary concerns. Rajan emphasises the significance of strong regulatory and technological precautions that safeguard people's personal data in an increasingly interconnected environment.
- **Online Harassment and Cyberbullying**: This has become more common due to the degree of privacy provided by social media sites. In order to stop such destructive behaviours and offer a safer online environment, Rajan

advocates for greater accountability and higher standards of ethics.

Opportunities

Global Connectivity: Digital communication technologies have transcended geographical boundaries, enabling individuals to connect and collaborate on a global scale. Rajan underscores the transformative potential of this interconnectedness for fostering cross-cultural understanding and international cooperation.

The Democratisation of Information: The internet has democratised access to information, empowering individuals to participate in public discourse and hold institutions accountable. Rajan emphasises the role of digital platforms in amplifying diverse voices and catalysing social change.

Innovation and Entrepreneurship: The digital economy has spurred innovation and entrepreneurship, creating new opportunities for economic growth and development.

Rajan draws attention to the revolutionary role that digital platforms and tech firms play in promoting economic empowerment and the creation of opportunities.

Better Communication Channels: Digital technologies have transformed communication channels by facilitating real-time engagement and linking us via a variety of social media platforms. In his exploration of opportunities for seamless interaction and collaboration in both personal and professional settings, Rajan looks at social networking, instant messaging, and video conferencing platforms.

In summary, the digital era offers many kinds of chances and difficulties for communication, influencing how we interact, connect, and work together with the globe. We obtained a greater comprehension of the challenges involved in navigating this changing environment and the necessity of embracing innovation, diversity, and responsible stewardship to fully realize the promise through the views of well-known Indian personality Raghuram Rajan.

Here's an example of another famous Indian personality and strategies for effective email communication, virtual meetings, and social media interaction:

Vineeta Singh, co-founder of Sugar Cosmetics, approaches effective communication as follows:

1. Email Communication

Strategy: Be clear, concise, and professional while showcasing personality and brand voice.

Example: Vineeta likely sends brief, purpose-driven emails. She might start with a direct subject line like "Next Steps for Our Product Launch" and keep her message clear, outlining key points and action steps while maintaining a friendly tone.

Tip: Always include a strong call to action at the end of the email, making it clear what you want the recipient to do next.

2. Virtual Meetings

Strategy: Create an engaging, interactive atmosphere that promotes team collaboration.

Example: In a virtual meeting with her Sugar Cosmetics team, Vineeta would likely set a clear agenda, ensure everyone has a chance to contribute, and use visuals or product samples to keep the meeting engaging. She might encourage a casual check-in at the start to build rapport before diving into business.

Tip: Keep meetings concise and focused, but also allocate time for questions and ideas to flow, promoting inclusivity.

3. Social Media Interaction:

Strategy: Leverage authenticity and community engagement to build brand loyalty.

Example: On platforms like Instagram, Vineeta often shares personal insights, business challenges, and behind-the-scenes content about Sugar Cosmetics, engaging her audience with authentic stories and interactive polls. She balances business updates with personal moments, making her relatable.

Tip: Use interactive features like polls, Q&As, and direct messages to maintain a two-way conversation with followers. Authenticity is key to creating trust and building a strong social media presence.

These strategies mirror Vineeta Singh's approach to communication: clear, engaging, and personable, whether it's through email, virtual meetings, or social media interactions.

Here's How You Can Do It Too

- **Get ready**: Create an agenda and send it out to participants ahead of time. To guarantee a fruitful conversation, establish roles and responsibilities.
- **Participation**: Encourage everyone in the audience to actively participate by requesting their opinions and suggestions. To encourage participation, make use of tools like polls and breakout rooms.
- **Respect Time**: Be mindful of participants' schedules by starting and concluding meetings on time. At the end of the meeting, summarise the main ideas and the next steps.
- **Social Media Interactions:** Ratan Tata's involvement on

social media sites such as Twitter has drawn attention due to his insightful posts and his interaction with his followers.

Effective Tactics for Boosting Social Media Engagement

- **Sincerity**: Share your own ideas and experiences with others to keep your conversations authentic. Steer clear of canned or spontaneous answers.
- **Engagement**: Retweet relevant details, reply to comments, start conversations about interesting subjects, and actively interact with your audience.
- **Thought Leadership**: To become a thought leader in your field, share insightful observations and extensive industry expertise. Address popular subjects and offer answers to often-encountered problems.

For Example:

Ratan Tata's email to stakeholders regarding a new initiative:

Subject: Launch of Sustainable Innovation Initiative

Dear Stakeholders,

I hope this email finds you well. I'm thrilled to announce the launch of our new Sustainable Innovation Initiative aimed at fostering environmentally conscious practices within our organisation.

Key Highlights:

- Introduction of eco-friendly packaging solutions.
- Implementation of energy-efficient technologies in manufacturing facilities.
- Collaboration with local communities for sustainable development projects.

Your support and collaboration are crucial as we embark on this journey towards a greener future. Please feel free to reach out with any questions or suggestions.

Warm regards,

Ratan Tata

By incorporating these strategies inspired by Ratan Tata's approach, individuals and organisations can enhance their communication effectiveness across email, virtual meetings, and social media platforms.

Digital Professionalism and Online Reputation Management

In the modern era of technology, where information spreads like wildfire and online interactions are more accepted, it is difficult to adequately emphasise the importance of digital etiquette and online reputation management.

It is crucial to know how to behave properly online and keep a positive digital reputation, regardless of whether you are a public person, a professional, or just an individual exploring the vast world of the internet.

The conventions, laws, and guidelines governing proper conduct in online communications and interactions are collectively referred to as digital etiquette or internet protocol. It involves using common sense, civility, and respect while interacting with others on digital media. Following digital etiquette ensures constructive communication and promotes positive interactions on social media and in email correspondence.

It's also crucial to protect one's online reputation, which is why following proper digital etiquette goes beyond simply being courteous. Your digital footprint is a component made up of your social media activity, posts, comments, and interactions. It reflects your online presence. Similar to how your actions and words affect other people's opinions about you in the actual world, this also applies to the digital sphere.

As a result, controlling your internet reputation is crucial to influencing how the public, prospective employers, colleagues, and peers view you. Dr Kiran Bedi is a well-known Indian celebrity who serves as a fantastic example of the significance of online reputation management and digital manners.

Renowned for her remarkable tenure as the first and highest-ranking female officer in the Indian Police Service (IPS), as well as her subsequent roles in governance and activism, Dr Bedi has navigated the digital landscape with grace and prudence.

Dr Bedi has always carried out herself with dignity and respect on the internet, even in the midst of criticism and controversy. She facilitates extensive use of social media platforms to voice her support for social problems, share her thoughts, and engage in insightful discussions with her followers.

Dr Bedi has developed a great online reputation that is consistent with her values and goals by upholding the ideas of transparency, empathy, and integrity in her digital etiquette. Furthermore, Dr Bedi is aware of how digital communication can influence social change and public opinion. By using strategic online interaction, she has proficiently strengthened her voice, gathered support for causes that are important to her, and cultivated significant conversations on matters of national significance.

Dr Bedi is an inspiration for how people may leverage the internet for a good while maintaining ethical standards since she focuses on digital etiquette and carefully manages her online reputation. In conclusion, in today's corresponding world, the significance of online reputation management and digital etiquette cannot be underestimated. Whether you're a well-known public figure like Dr Kiran Bedi or merely an ordinary individual navigating the digital world, it's critical to have a polite online presence and protect your online reputation.

You may create a positive digital footprint that represents your goals and values by following the rules of digital etiquette, encouraging pleasant interactions, and upholding honesty and integrity in your online identity. Dr Bedi's example shows that using grace and mindfulness when navigating the digital space can lead to meaningful connections, opportunities, and impact in both personal and professional spheres.

Top 3 Frustrations

- **Overcoming Miscommunication:** Non-verbal cues that are crucial in conveying tone and intent are frequently absent in digital communication, which can result in miscommunication and misconceptions.
- **Overload of Information:** It might be challenging to prioritise and respond appropriately due to the sheer volume of texts, emails, and notifications.
- **Absence of Engagement:** Digital platforms can occasionally give off an impersonal impression, making it harder to stay engaged and build deep relationships with people.

Top 3 Fears

- **Fear of Miscommunication:** Worry that by not interacting face-to-face and using non-verbal cues, you may be misunderstood or misread.

- **Fear of Being Ignored or Overlooked:** Fear that communications may be misinterpreted or undervalued as a result of being lost in the digital cacophony or not obtaining a prompt response.
- **Fear of Privacy and Security Breaches:** Anxiety over the potential for personal or sensitive information to be exposed or hacked in digital communication platforms.

Top 3 Ways to Overcome Digital Communication Challenges

- **Clarity and Precision**: Be clear and concise in your communication. Use simple language and structure your communication to ensure your intent is easily understood. Avoid jargon and difficult terms.
- **Utilise Multiple Channels:** Use a mix of communication channels to enhance understanding and engagement. For example, follow up important emails with a brief video call or use instant messaging for quick clarifications.
- **Build Digital Etiquette:** Develop and follow good digital communication practices, such as timely responses, respectful language, and active listening. Encourage others to do the same to foster a respectful and efficient communication environment.

8

Overcoming Communication Barriers

The foundation of human interaction, communicating, is essential for building connections, communicating thoughts, and accomplishing shared objectives. Effective communication challenges, however, may hinder understanding, lead to misinterpretations, and hamper progress. Using the experiences of well-known Indian personalities as examples, we will explore numerous communication obstacles and solutions in this chapter.

Understanding Communication Barriers

Different languages, cultural backgrounds, and physical, psychological, and technological hurdles are just a few ways in which barriers to communication might appear.

Speaking different languages or dialects hinders people from understanding one another. This is known as a language barrier. Different cultural customs, attitudes, and communication styles give rise to barriers among cultures, which can cause misunderstandings and disagreements. Physical obstacles like bad infrastructure, noise, or distance might interfere with communication. How signals are expressed and received are affected by psychological obstacles like biases, prejudices, and emotional states. Limitations or failures in communication platforms and equipment give rise to technological hurdles.

Strategies for Overcoming Communication Barriers

- **Active Listening**: Listening effectively is the first step in effective communication. To ensure reciprocated understanding, encourage transparent communication, offer clarification, and provide comments.
- **Cultural Sensitivity**: Develop an understanding and respect for numerous points of view held by different cultures. To account for cultural differences in communication, build an understanding of cultural differences, refrain from expecting anything that you do, and adapt your communication approach.
- **Clear and Concise Communication**: To minimise confusion and unpredictability, speak clearly, stay away from jargon, and express yourself clearly and precisely.
- **Empathy and Understanding**: As you establish rapport and trust, envision yourself in the other person's shoes, understand their point of view, and show empathy.
- **Feedback Mechanisms**: Develop feedback mechanisms for receiving feedback, handling issues, and assessing understanding. Promote open channels of communication to enable the exchange of helpful criticism.

- **Adaptability**: Be flexible and adaptable in your communication approach. Tailor your message and delivery method based on the needs, preferences, and capabilities of your audience.

Dr APJ Abdul Kalam

Through his inclusive leadership style and successful communication methods, Dr APJ Abdul Kalam, commonly referred to as the "People's President" and the "Missile Man of India," demonstrates how to overcome communication hurdles. Although Dr Kalam's training was in aeronautical engineering, he had an amazing ability to inspire people from a wide range of backgrounds with his vision for a better India.

Highlighting simplicity and clarity was one of Dr Kalam's notable communication techniques. His talent was explaining difficult scientific ideas in simple terms that both specialists and laypeople could understand. Dr Kalam's talks were inspirational, sincere, and devoid of linguistic or cultural complexities, whether he was speaking to legislators, scientists, or students.

Moreover, Dr Kalam's humility and approachability endeared him to people from all walks of life. He actively listened to others, valued their perspectives, and encouraged participation, creating an inclusive environment where communication flourished. Despite holding the highest office in the country, Dr Kalam remained accessible and approachable, breaking down hierarchical barriers and fostering open dialogue.

His unique blend of scientific expertise, humility, and deep empathy set him apart as an extraordinary figure in India's history. What made Dr Kalam truly outstanding was his ability to communicate complex ideas with simplicity and clarity, making science and technology accessible to all.

Dr Kalam's growth as a leader was closely tied to his exceptional communication skills. His speeches and writings were always infused with optimism, hope, and a sense of purpose. Dr. Kalam was not just a brilliant scientist. He was also a remarkable storyteller who could weave together technical knowledge and moral lessons in a way that resonated deeply with his audience.

This ability to communicate effectively allowed him to gain the trust and respect of millions, helping him to lead major scientific projects and inspire a nation. His words had the power to motivate, educate, and unite people towards a common goal of national development.

Unlock Success with These Key Communication Skills

- **Inspiring and Motivating Others**: Just as Dr Kalam inspired a generation through his words, effective communication can help you inspire and motivate those around you. Whether you're leading a team, mentoring someone, or simply sharing ideas, clear and positive communication can encourage others to reach their full potential.
- **Building Trust and Relationships**: Dr Kalam's ability to connect with people on a personal level through his communication was a key factor in his success. In everyday life, using clear, empathetic, and honest communication can help you build trust and strong relationships with others, be it in personal or professional settings.

Communication works for those who work at it.

—**John Powell**

In summary, overcoming challenges to communication is critical to promoting progress, cooperation, and understanding. Through the implementation of techniques like attentive listening, cultural awareness, and flexibility, people can overcome gaps and foster significant relationships. By taking inspiration from role models such as Dr APJ Abdul Kalam, we can gain important insights about leadership and successful communication.

Breaking Barriers: Navigating Communication Challenges for Professional Success

The foundation of being successful in both personal and professional endeavours is effective communication. However, a number of obstacles frequently stand in the way of effective and transparent communication, which can result in miscommunication, disputes, and lost opportunities.

Using the life of a well-known Indian personality as an example, we will explore frequent communication hurdles in this part of the chapter and how they affect relationships and career success.

Mahatma Gandhi, known as the "Father of the Nation," demonstrated outstanding communication skills throughout his life. His ability to inspire millions, relate to individuals from all backgrounds and guide India towards independence through nonviolent struggle makes him a perfect subject for researching communication barriers and their effects.

Cultural Barriers: Mahatma Gandhi had several cultural obstacles when fighting for India's independence, especially when trying to unite the differences between diverse ethnic and religious groups.

He faced pushback and criticism from a variety of sources

because of his emphasis on non-violence and unity in the context of firmly established societal standards.

Misunderstandings, a lack of confidence, and conflict caused due to cultural differences may hinder collaboration and development. Mahatma Gandhi successfully brought various groups together to achieve a common objective by eliminating these obstacles via respectful and inclusive communication.

Language Barriers: Mahatma Gandhi encountered linguistic difficulties in India's linguistically diverse landscape as a national leader striving for reform. Many languages were spoken in various parts of the country, making it difficult to mobilise the general population through effective interaction. Mahatma Gandhi overcame this difficulty by using simple language that was understandable in both his writings and speeches, which helped individuals from a variety of linguistic backgrounds to understand his message.

Socio-economic Barriers: Mahatma Gandhi challenged long-standing discrimination in Indian society through his campaigns for social justice and economic equality.

His focus on strengthening the underprivileged, like labourers, and untouchables, put the operating power structures in danger and pushed back against them.

Inequalities and a lack of fair communication might result from socio-economic constraints. Mahatma Gandhi intended to break down these barriers and encourage open discussion for the improvement of society by elevating the voices of the marginalised and promoting discourse across social strategy.

Emotional Obstacles: During his time, as a leader, Mahatma Gandhi faced emotional obstacles in the form of resentment, opposition, and personal assaults. He had to deal with difficult emotions and keep his cool under stress because of his steadfast commitment to non-violence and determination during times of hardship.

Conflicts can intensify, empathy can become less effective, and trust can be undermined by emotional barriers. In times of tremendous challenges, Mahatma Gandhi was capable of getting past emotional barriers and creating long-lasting relationships through his ability to connect with his opponents, respond compassionately, and maintain his beliefs.

This personal story is an important source of information about the dynamics of communication challenges and the way they influence connections and professional achievement. Cultural, linguistic, financial, and emotional barriers can be identified and addressed, allowing people to develop inclusive ways to communicate that encourage collaboration, understanding, and positive transformation.

Remembering Mahatma Gandhi's legacy helps us as we negotiate the challenges of communication in a world that is becoming more interconnected with the transformative power of effective communication while shaping our collective future.

Overcoming Barriers: Practical Exercises and Techniques

It has grown increasingly essential to navigate obstacles like interpersonal problems, linguistic limitations, and cultural differences in today's interconnected world. Overcoming these obstacles is essential for effective collaboration and interaction, whether in the business setting, in educational settings, or in daily encounters. In order to deal with these challenges meticulously and effectively, this part of the chapter tries to provide helpful exercises and strategies. Communities gain from cultural diversity. However, there may be challenges with interaction at times.

Individuals must first acknowledge and fully understand cultural differences in order to overcome them. Here are some practical exercises to help with this:

- **Workshops on Cultural Understanding**: Organise discussions where attendees exchange stories and perspectives on their own cultures. This encourages compassion and understanding.
- Encourage participants in cross-cultural role-playing to carry through circumstances which include cultural misunderstandings. This promotes empathy and the development of problem-solving abilities.
- **Cultural Immersion Activities**: To experience a first-hand glimpse at the diversity in our environment, we can engage in activities like visiting cultural events or sampling cuisine from various cultures.
- **Overcoming Language Obstacles**: Although they can obstruct efficient communication, language obstacles can be surmounted with the appropriate techniques. Examples of useful methods are:
    - **Language Exchange Programmes**: Assist reciprocal language learning by matching speakers of various languages.
    - **Language Instruction**: Provide instruction in languages that are suited to the requirements of particular groups, emphasising words and expressions that are crucial for communication.

  - **Translation Tools**: Introduce and demonstrate the use of translation tools and resources to aid communication in multilingual environments.

- **Resolving Interpersonal Conflicts:** Conflicting interests, communication styles, and personality differences are only a few of the causes of interpersonal problems.
- Engage in active listening throughout conversations by using strategies like summarising and paraphrasing to make sure everyone understands each other.
- **Conduct Conflict Resolution Workshops**: Teach participants how to resolve conflicts through compromise, mediation, and negotiation. Create role-playing situations based on typical interpersonal disputes and lead participants through productive techniques for resolving disputes.
- **Integration of Exercises and Techniques**: It is crucial to incorporate these exercises and techniques into a complete approach in order to maximise their effectiveness.
- **Determine Needs**: Determine the particular obstacles and difficulties that people or groups are facing in a particular situation.
- **Customise Solutions**: Tailor exercises and techniques to address the identified needs and preferences of participants.
- **Continuous Evaluation**: Regularly evaluate the effectiveness of implemented strategies and adjust as needed to ensure ongoing improvement.
- **Promote Diversity and Inclusion**: Foster a culture of diversity and inclusion where individuals feel valued and respected for their unique backgrounds and perspectives.

Awareness, compassion, and practical skills are needed to overcome obstacles, including language hurdles, cultural differences, and conflicts between individuals. Both individuals and organisations may enhance understanding, communication, and collaboration among one another by offering tasks and procedures that are specific to their setting. Not only can embracing diversity improve our relationships, but it also helps create a more harmonious and inclusive society when obstacles are actively removed.

9

Understanding Empathy and Emotional Intelligence in Effective Communication

Emotional intelligence and empathy are essential components of effective communication. This chapter explores the importance of empathy and emotional intelligence in creating lasting relationships by delving into their complex dynamics.

Understanding Empathy

Effective communication depends largely on empathy, which is commonly defined as having the ability to understand and connect with another person's emotions. It includes not just being aware of the emotions of other individuals but also responding to them in a considerate and understanding way. The concepts of cognitive empathy, or seeing things from their point of view, and emotional empathy, or feeling and sharing their feelings, are both included in the concept of empathy.

The Importance of Empathy in Communication

In communication, empathy is essential because it promotes mutual trust, understanding, and a sense of togetherness. Empathetic communicators create an atmosphere where people are acknowledged, heard, and feel valued. In both personal and professional conversations, empathetic communication encourages collaboration, cooperation, and dispute resolution.

Developing Empathy Skills

Even though compassion can come effortlessly to some people, it can also be taught and increased with practice. Empathetic communication requires taking on new perspectives, active listening, and awareness of non-verbal signs. Through the development of these abilities, people can become more skilled at navigating complicated interpersonal dynamics and establishing deeper connections with others.

Emotional Intelligence and Communication

To be emotionally intelligent (EI) means to be able to identify, comprehend, and control one's own feelings as well as those of others. High emotional intelligence is necessary for effective communication because it allows people to control their emotions, empathise with others, and modify their communication style to fit various situations and personalities.

The Four Components of Emotional Intelligence

Leading expert on emotional intelligence, Daniel Goleman, distinguished four essential elements of EI: relationship management, social awareness, self-regulation, and self-awareness. Based on these elements, people can navigate interpersonal encounters with sincerity, empathy, and sensitivity. These elements are the cornerstones of good communication.

Enhancing Emotional Intelligence for Better Communication

Self-awareness initiatives, self-reflection, and continuous personal development are all necessary for increasing emotional intelligence. A deeper comprehension of one's own emotions as well as those of others can help people become more adept communicators who can forge stronger bonds and handle conflict with grace and empathy.

Empathy and Emotional Intelligence in Leadership Communication

Empathy and emotional intelligence are essential qualities for leaders. Authentic and empathetic communication, creating a welcoming and inclusive work atmosphere, and being aware of the needs and worries of their team members are all ways that effective leaders show empathy. Through clear and compassionate communication, leaders can motivate their colleagues, foster trust, and advance organisational success by utilizing their emotional intelligence.

Effective communication is essential in personal as well as professional circumstances, and it starts with empathy and emotional intelligence. Building deeper connections, encouraging teamwork, and navigating interpersonal dynamics with grace and understanding are all possible for those who cultivate these traits and incorporate them into their communication habits.

Indian Entrepreneurs' Views on the Significance of Empathy and Emotional Intelligence

In today's ever-changing business world, effective communication is essential. But beyond language and speech abilities, emotional intelligence and empathy are critical for creating meaningful relationships and achieving organisational goals.

This part of the chapter describes the role that emotional intelligence and empathy play in communication abilities, providing perspectives from the lives of well-known Indian businesspeople.

Understanding Emotional Intelligence: The Power of Empathy

The capacity to comprehend and experience another person's emotions is known as empathy, and it enables people to emotionally bond with one another.

Social awareness, relationship management, self-regulation, and self-awareness are all included in emotional intelligence.

When combined, these traits provide people with the ability to handle interpersonal dynamics with tact and wisdom.

The Confluence of Communication, Emotional Intelligence, and Empathy

Establishing relationships, trust, and being mindful of the needs and perspectives of others are all important components of effective communication. Such communication is based on empathy and emotional intelligence, which promote meaningful interactions and teamwork.

These attributes enable business owners to communicate with significance and honesty, whether it's while pitching a vision to stakeholders, settling disputes within teams, or comprehending client feedback.

Practical Examples from Indian Entrepreneurs

Aman Gupta, co-founder of boAt, exemplifies empathetic management through his hands-on, people-first leadership style.

Here's a practical example:

During the COVID-19 Pandemic, which disrupted global supply chains and created uncertainty, Aman focused on his employees' well-being and mental health. He introduced flexible work-from-home policies and prioritised frequent check-ins, both to ensure the team's physical health and to offer emotional support. This helped foster a sense of security among his employees during a stressful time.

He also showed empathy in business decisions by understanding the struggles of consumers and offering affordable products without compromising on quality or helping.

Azim Premji, the founder of Wipro Limited, is renowned not only for his business acumen but also for his exceptional emotional intelligence (EI). His ability to understand and manage emotions—both his own and those of others—has been pivotal in navigating challenges and driving the company's success.

When Wipro underwent significant restructuring to adapt to the changing tech landscape, Premji faced resistance from employees concerned about job security and the future direction of the company.

Emotional Intelligence Strategies Used

- **Active Listening:** Premji hosted town hall meetings where he encouraged open dialogue. He actively listened to employees' concerns, validating their feelings and ensuring they felt heard.

- **Empathy:** Understanding the emotional climate of his workforce, he shared personal stories of his own challenges during times of change, fostering a connection and demonstrating that he empathised with their fears.
- **Transparent Communication:** He communicated the reasons for the restructuring transparently, outlining how it would position Wipro for future growth. This openness helped to alleviate anxiety and build trust among employees.

Piyush Bansal, Co-founder and CEO of Lenskart, has been instrumental in fostering a culture of empathy within Lenskart, one of India's leading eyewear brands. Here's how he effectively uses communication skills to cultivate empathy in the corporate environment:

Open-Door Policy

Communication Skill: **Active Listening**

Bansal encourages employees to voice their concerns and suggestions by maintaining an open-door policy. He regularly engages in one-on-one meetings with team members, actively listening to their challenges and experiences. This approach not only makes employees feel valued but also fosters trust and transparency.

Employee Feedback Mechanisms

Communication Skill: **Constructive Feedback**

Bansal implements regular feedback sessions where employees can share their thoughts on workplace culture and management practices. He emphasises the importance of constructive feedback, encouraging teams to express their ideas and feelings about their work environment, leading to improvements based on real employee insights.

Inclusive Decision-Making

Communication Skill: **Collaborative Communication**

Bansal involves employees in key decision-making processes, seeking their input on new initiatives or company policies. By valuing diverse perspectives and fostering inclusive discussions, he creates a sense of belonging and shared ownership among team members.

Indra Nooyi: Communicating with Authenticity

The former CEO of PepsiCo, Indra Nooyi, is praised for her leadership approach, which is grounded in emotional intelligence. Throughout her tenure, she shared both triumphs and challenges with stakeholders in a humble and open manner. Employees, investors, and customers all responded favourably to Nooyi's ability to be vulnerable while upholding a firm vision, which helped in building a culture of trust and loyalty within the company.

Effective communication is essential in the quick-paced world of entrepreneurship. But beyond following up on verbal and non-verbal signs, emotional intelligence and empathy are essential for creating deep connections and producing favourable results. These attributes can be used to overcome obstacles, create resilient companies, and have a long-lasting effect on society, as illustrated by Indian businesspeople like Ratan Tata, Kiran Mazumdar-Shaw and Indra Nooyi. Entrepreneurs who embrace empathy and emotional intelligence are able to inspire, motivate, and lead with authenticity in addition to communicating successfully.

Cultivating Empathy and Emotional Intelligence: Lessons from Indian Influencers

Empathy and emotional intelligence have become vital traits in today's interconnected society for negotiating complicated social dynamics and building deep connections. The foundation for mastering these abilities is effective communication, which enables people to comprehend and relate to the feelings and experiences of others.

Taking cues from well-known Indian leaders in a range of fields, this chapter delves into activities, case studies, and real-world applications meant to improve communication skills and empathy.

Activities to Improve Emotional Intelligence and Empathy

- **Role-Playing Perspectives**: Split participants into pairs and give each pair a scenario in which they have to role-play several points of view. In one scenario, for instance, there would be a disagreement amongst co-workers, and each participant would represent the viewpoint of a different co-worker.
- To come to a resolution, encourage parties to communicate clearly, listen attentively, and understand the other side's point of view.
- **Reflective Listening Circles**: Establish small groups in which members alternately share their own struggles or experiences. Paraphrasing and summarizing the speaker's thoughts and experiences is the listener's job when engaging in reflective listening.
- Through deeper comprehension and validation of others' feelings, this practice develops empathy.
- **Empathy Mapping:** Provide unfinished diagrams of empathy with spaces for influences, ideas, feelings, and actions to participants. Give them a scenario to work through or your own experience, and have them fill in the map with the motivations, feelings, and actions of the people

in it. By prompting participants to think about numerous perspectives and underlying emotions, this visual exercise improves empathy.

Tools to Enhance Emotional Intelligence

- **Conflict Resolution in the Workplace**: Consider an instance where disagreements among co-workers regarding how to tackle a project have caused friction and conflict. Facilitate a discussion between participants about assertive expression, compromise, active listening, and other effective communication techniques.
- Utilise the successful alternative dispute resolution techniques of Indian entrepreneur and motivational speaker Shiv Khera, who is well-known for his proficiency in people skills and leadership.
- **Navigating Cultural Differences:** Give an example of a circumstance where cultural differences produce confusion between persons from various backgrounds.
- Lead a conversation about empathy, cultural awareness, and the significance of changing communication methods to overcome cultural differences.

Priyanka Chopra Jonas, an Indian actress and UNICEF Goodwill Ambassador, shares her experiences and calls for global understanding and cultural acceptance.

- **Supporting Mental Health Awareness:** Describe a situation in which a friend or co-worker confides in someone about their mental health issues.

Assist participants in investigating ways to provide support without passing judgment, empathic answers, and active listening strategies.

Take a cue from Dr. Anjali Chhabria, an Indian psychologist and mental health advocate who works to destigmatise mental health issues via compassionate education and communication.

Practical Examples from Indian Influencers

Ratan Tata: Philanthropy and Social Responsibility

He was a well-known Indian philanthropist and industrialist who, through his dedication to social initiatives, exhibited empathy and emotional intelligence. His ability to effectively communicate with stakeholders and communities showed that he genuinely cared about the welfare of society, which promotes cooperation and trust.

Sudha Murthy: Using Storytelling to Strengthen Communities

Author and philanthropist Sudha Murthy advocates for social change by using storytelling as a method to engage a variety of audiences. People are inspired to empathise with others' experiences and contribute to good development by her ability to convey empathy and emotional depth via narratives.

A.R. Rahman: Building a Cultural Bridge through Music

Legendary composer and musician Rahman's music fosters empathy and understanding across varied communities by transcending cultural boundaries.

His musical pieces elicit strong feelings and connect with listeners globally, demonstrating the ability of artistic expression to foster empathy and promote empathy and emotional intelligence.

Conclusion

We've accomplished important insights on how to improve compassion and emotional intelligence via successful communication by incorporating activities, scenarios, and real-world examples.

By developing these abilities, people may make more meaningful connections, handle tricky social situations, and influence positive social change in both their personal and professional lives. In many contexts, including athletics, trust-building and the development of deep bonds depend heavily on empathic communication.

People who communicate with empathy show that they are understanding, compassionate, and genuinely concerned about the feelings and viewpoints of others. This fosters an atmosphere of respect and support for one another in addition to strengthening interpersonal ties.

Several instances involving Indian athletes demonstrate the significant influence that compassionate communication has on both their professional lives and the communities they serve.

Sania, a pioneering tennis player, has not only excelled in her sport but has also dedicated herself to advocating for women's representation in athletics.

Through her mentorship programs, she engages young female athletes with empathy, sharing her own challenges and victories to inspire them. Sania actively uses social media platforms to address issues such as gender inequality in sports and advocating for equal opportunities and pay.

Her ability to communicate compassionately has fostered a supportive community, encouraging many young girls to pursue their dreams in sports.

Rohit Sharma, the captain of the Indian cricket team, exemplifies the power of empathetic communication in leadership.

He creates an environment of open dialogue within the team, ensuring that each player's voice is heard and respected.

Rohit often shares personal stories and experiences, promoting a culture of camaraderie and trust. After matches, he frequently engages with fans, expressing gratitude for their support and sharing insights into the team's journey.

His compassionate approach not only strengthens team dynamics but also builds a loyal fan base, as supporters feel connected to the players and their experiences.

Together, these athletes demonstrate how compassionate communication can significantly impact both their professional journeys and the communities they influence.

Furthermore, the influence of compassionate communication goes beyond specific athletes to encompass sports organisations and broader communities.

An excellent instance is the non-profit Akshaya Patra Foundation, which feeds school children in India midday meals. The Indian spiritual master, Swami Prabhupada established the foundation, which places a strong emphasis on the value of compassion and empathy in resolving social issues.

The Akshaya Patra Foundation received fame and a great deal of support for its initiatives to fight hunger and advance education for disadvantaged children by using powerful communication techniques that put empathy and understanding first.

In conclusion, the foundation for establishing meaningful connections and constructing trust in sports and other domains is sympathetic communication.

In their particular domains, Indian athletes like Mahindra Singh Dhoni and P.V. Sindhu serve as prime examples of the transforming power of empathy, showing how comprehension, kindness, and sincere concern can bring people together to achieve shared goals.

By embracing empathetic communication, athletes, organisations, and communities can create environments that nurture personal growth, mutual respect, and collective success.

Top 3 Frustrations in Communication Skills:

- **Misunderstandings and Miscommunication**: People often feel frustrated when their messages are misunderstood or misinterpreted, leading to conflicts and confusion.
- **Inability to Convey Emotions Effectively**: Many struggle to express their emotions clearly, which can result in a lack of emotional connection and empathy from others.
- **Difficulty in Active Listening**: Some find it challenging to truly listen and engage with others, missing out on crucial details and emotional cues in conversations.

Top 3 Fears in Communication Skills:

- **Fear of Judgment or Criticism**: Individuals often fear being judged or criticised for their communication style, ideas, or emotional expressions, leading to anxiety and reluctance to communicate openly.
- **Fear of Vulnerability**: Sharing emotions and personal thoughts can make people feel vulnerable, which they fear might be exploited or misunderstood.
- **Fear of Conflict**: Many people avoid difficult conversations due to the fear of creating or escalating conflicts, leading to unresolved issues and strained relationships.

Top 3 Ways to Overcome Frustrations and Fears with Empathy and Emotional Intelligence:

- **Practice Active Listening**: Focus entirely on the speaker, avoid interrupting, and reflect on what is being said before responding. This helps in understanding the speaker's emotions and perspective, reducing misunderstandings and building trust.

- **Develop Self-Awareness:** Regularly reflect on your own emotions, triggers, and communication patterns. Journaling and mindfulness practices can be helpful. Increased self-awareness helps you regulate your emotions and respond more thoughtfully in conversations, reducing the fear of vulnerability and criticism.
- **Enhance Empathy:** Put yourself in the other person's shoes, actively consider their feelings and perspectives, and express understanding and compassion. Empathy bridges emotional gaps and fosters stronger, more meaningful connections, alleviating the fear of judgment and conflict.

9

Crisis Communication

Crisis communication is an important component of public relations since it aims to maintain and protect an organisation's reputation in difficult times.

Effective communication with stakeholders, such as employees, clients, investors, and the media in general, is critical for addressing the issue and reducing its adverse effects.

- **Recognising the Crisis:** Determine the type and scope of the crisis. Ascertain what or who was impacted, what occurred, and why it occurred.
- **Evaluate the possible outcomes**: Consider the potential effects of the crisis on operations, finances, reputation, and stakeholders.
- **Form a crisis management team**: To plan how to respond, put together a cross-functional team with clear roles and responsibilities.

Developing an Approach to Communication

- **Specify Goals**: Establish specific objectives for your communications, such as upholding openness, safeguarding stakeholders, and keeping reputation.
- **Decide on the Major Points**: Formulate understanding and consistent comments that address stakeholders' concerns, along with illustrating the organisation's commitment to finding a resolution.
- **Choose Suitable Routes for Communication**: Select distribution techniques that will effectively reach your target audience, such as direct communication, social media, press releases, and website updates.

Carrying Out the Communication Strategy

- **Take Immediate Action**: In order to show proactive management and reassure stakeholders, communicate right after the crisis.
- Provide accurate and timely information to stakeholders on a regular basis, even if there are no notable happenings.
- **Monitor the Media's Coverage**: Keep an eye on news coverage and social media discussions to effectively regulate the message and counter false information.
- **Give Spokespersons More Authority**: Select experienced spokespeople to communicate with the media.
- **Tailoring Responses to Changing Conditions**: Pay attention to detail. It is critical to incorporate stakeholder feedback while improving communication approaches. Be open and honest.

- **Accept Your Mistakes:** If you've made mistakes or gone short, admit it and demonstrate your willingness to improve.
- **Be Prepared for the Long Journey**: Plan for ongoing communication and reputation management following the original crisis to restore credibility and confidence.

Example: Crisis Communication Plan for a Data Breach Incident

1. Understanding the Crisis:

Nature: A cybersecurity breach compromised customer data, including personal information and payment details.

Extent: The breach affects thousands of customers who may be at risk of identity theft or financial fraud.

2. Communication Strategy:

The goals are to minimise reputational harm, restore confidence, and guarantee that impacted customers receive fast and accurate information.

Key Takeaways: Express regret for the security lapse, reassure clients of safeguards, and offer guidance on how to keep their data safe.

Channels: Send emails to impacted customers, post FAQs to the firm website, issue a news statement, and interact on social media.

3. Implementation:

Swift Response: As soon as possible, inform clients via email and social media about the breach, stressing the company's dedication to their security. Update customers on a regular basis about the status of the investigation, security improvements, and available options for assistance.

Media Monitoring: Keep an eye on social media and news sources for any mentions of the breach, and take quick action to address any concerns and rectify any misinformation that may arise.

Spokesman: As the main point of contact for customer contacts and media queries, appoint the Chief Information Security Officer (CISO).

4. Adaptation:

Feedback: Pay attention to the opinions and concerns of your customers and take appropriate action by providing more avenues for communication and support.

Transparency: Describe the breach's cause, the actions taken to lessen its effects, and the precautions put in place to ensure that such breaches don't happen again.

Long-Term Planning: Create a long-term cybersecurity and communication plan that includes preventive customer outreach, staff training, and frequent security audits.

To sum up, proactive and open communication during a crisis is essential to addressing stakeholder concerns and safeguarding the organisation's reputation. Organisations may successfully traverse crises and emerge stronger by comprehending the situation, creating a communication strategy, carrying out the plan, and responding to input.

In times of crisis, good communication is essential to preserving order, guaranteeing security, and informing the public with correct information.

One cannot stress the value of communication during times of crisis in India more than in many other regions of the world.

Effective and prompt communication is essential for handling any emergency and lessening its effects, be it a natural disaster, pandemic, or societal unrest.

Importance of Effective Communication during Crisis Situations:

- **Information Transmission**: In order to make sound decisions during a crisis, people want timely, reliable information. The public is guaranteed to receive correct information via efficient communication channels, reducing confusion and panic.
- **Public Safety:** Clear communication allows authorities to better advise those who have been impacted about safety precautions, evacuation routes, and other critical instructions. This may lessen the amount of casualties and property damage.
- **Building Trust:** Open and honest communication strengthens connections between the public and the authorities. Individuals who believe information is being delivered honestly and transparently are more likely to follow directions and collaborate, which benefits overall response efforts.
- **Crisis Management**: The several agencies and stakeholders participating in the crisis management process must coordinate their response activities, and this requires effective communication. Communication channels that are clear promote quick decision-making and resource allocation, ensuring that all parties involved are informed and aligned on strategies to address the crisis efficiently.

- **Reputation Management**: How authorities handle communication during a crisis can significantly impact their reputation. By providing accurate information and demonstrating empathy towards those affected, organisations can maintain or even enhance their reputation in the long run.
- **Mitigating Rumours and Misinformation**: During crises, misinformation can spread rapidly, causing further chaos and hindering response efforts. Effective communication helps combat misinformation by providing authoritative sources of information.
- **Addressing Public Concerns**: Crises often lead to heightened public concern and anxiety. Effective communication allows authorities to address these concerns promptly, providing reassurance and reducing fear and uncertainty.

Example: Mahatma Gandhi during India's Independence Movement

Mahatma Gandhi, the leader of the nation of India's fight against British rule, provided a great illustration of the importance of effective communication in emergency situations.

His ability to inspire millions of people for non-violent protest was primarily because of his professional use of efficient communication strategies. Gandhi utilised a range of media techniques to communicate his message and generate public support throughout the independence fight.

He connected with people from all walks of life through his effortless, plain, and deeply motivated speeches, writings, and emails.

Gandhi used massive demonstrations, such as the 1930 Salt March, as one of his most visible communication strategies. Gandhi launched a 240-mile march to protest the British salt monopoly.

He accomplished this through legislation, but he also drew the attention of the worldwide press, effectively communicating the dire circumstances of the Indian people under colonialism.

Gandhi's emphasis on non-violent discussion and compassion for his opponents contributed significantly to the preservation of discipline and coherence within the independence movement.

Gandhi garnered domestic and worldwide respect and admiration by continuously encouraging his supporters to maintain discipline and peace in the face of British government brutality and repression.

Gandhi extended his message across the country through print media and grassroots organisations, in addition to public lectures and actions. His ashrams became centres for educating activists about non-violent protest, and his periodicals as well, *Young India* and *Harijan*, operated as places of worship.

Mahatma Gandhi's ability to communicate effectively was critical in inspiring Indian people and ensuring our independence. His ability to provide a morally compelling and clear message during a crisis is a classic example of good communication in challenging situations.

To summarise, effective communication during a crisis is critical for maintaining confidence, controlling the crisis's overall repercussions and ensuring public safety.

Mahatma Gandhi and other historical figures may teach us about the transformative power of communication during uncertain and difficult times. To maintain confidence and trust, transparent and empathetic communication is necessary for effective crisis management.

Honesty, transparency, and empathy have been prioritised in the crisis management tactics of a number of Indian organisations and people.

Let's delve into some notable case studies that highlight these principles:

Tata Group: As a result of the acquisition of Jaguar Land Rover and the worldwide economic slump, Tata Motors encountered considerable difficulties during the 2008 financial crisis. When it came to communicating openly, Ratan Tata, the Chairman of the Tata Group at the time, acknowledged the challenges the organisation was facing and outlined steps to overcome them.

Tata Motors was able to successfully manoeuvre through the crisis and maintain public trust by being transparent about the concerns and interacting with stakeholders.

Zomato: During the COVID-19 pandemic in 2020, Zomato, one of India's top meal delivery services, came under fire for hygiene issues. The CEO of Zomato, Deepinder Goyal, communicated sympathetically and swiftly to reassure clients of the company's strict safety protocols. By openly addressing concerns and providing transparent updates on hygiene protocols, Zomato restored customer confidence and maintained its market reputation.

Kerala Government: The state government, led by Chief Minister Pinarayi Vijayan, displayed excellent crisis management during the 2018 Kerala floods by using open lines of communication. To offer real-time updates on rescue operations, relief efforts, and safety precautions, the administration leveraged news conferences and social media platforms.

The Kerala government coordinated disaster response in an efficient manner and received worldwide praise for its open communication strategy by encouraging individuals to engage in discourse and using empathy in their messaging.

Air India: The Mangalore air tragedy in 2010 left Air India in a precarious situation with a high death toll. In addition to swiftly addressing the media and the public, expressing condolences, and stating the airline's commitment to safety and inquiry, Arvind Jadhav, the Chairman and Managing Director of Air India at the time, embodied transparent communication. Air India preserved its brand during the catastrophe by emphasising compassion and openness in its communications.

Infosys: Leading provider of IT services, Infosys, faced a crisis in 2019 after internal whistle-blowers claimed to have discovered financial irregularities and unethical behaviour.

Infosys CEO Salil Parekh responded in a straightforward manner, acknowledging the claims right away and starting an internal probe. Infosys proved its dedication to moral behaviour and won back investor confidence by candidly addressing the issues brought up by stakeholders and pledging to be accountable and honest.

Conclusion

Retaining credibility, trust, and resilience during a crisis depends critically on open and compassionate communication. The efficacy of emphasising transparency, candour, and empathy in crisis management methods is demonstrated by the case studies of the Tata Group, Zomato, Kerala Government, Air India, and Infosys.

Through assimilating these models, entities and individuals can augment their crisis communication methodologies. Crafting crisis communication plans and responding to emergencies requires a comprehensive understanding of guidelines to effectively mitigate risks and manage the situation. Here's a detailed breakdown, along with examples:

Preparation and Planning: Gather important players from the legal, HR, PR, and senior management departments.

Identify roles, duties, communication protocols, and escalation procedures and include them in a crisis communication strategy.

To make sure the team is equipped to handle emergencies effectively, conduct frequent training sessions and role-plays.

Example: A multinational company forms a crisis communication team with members from its PR department, legal counsel, and executive leadership to prepare for possible crises.

They hold a quarterly review and update session for the crisis communication strategy, as well as an annual crisis simulation exercise to gauge their level of readiness.

Risk Assessment and Monitoring: Determine whether a crisis is approaching and evaluate how it might affect the stakeholders, operations, and reputation of the organisation. Watch for warning signs of forthcoming emergencies on social media, in the news, and from other sources.

Create procedures for judging a crisis's urgency and figuring out the right amount of assistance. In order to identify possible issues with food safety, a food manufacturing company, for instance, periodically tracks customer reviews on social media sites and carries out market research.

The company's crisis communication team gets notified on social media when reports of food-borne illnesses linked to one of its products emerge. They look into the claims and act quickly.

Transparency and Accountability: Provide timely and accurate information about the situation and its effects to stakeholders in order to demonstrate transparency. Admit errors or shortfalls, take ownership of the situation, and show that you are committed to fixing it. To preserve credibility and confidence, be open and honest in your communications with staff, clients, investors, and other stakeholders.

Example: A technology company will publicly acknowledge a data breach, apologise to the impacted customers, detail the security measures implemented to protect client data, and prevent similar incidents in the future. In order to allay worries and reassure stakeholders of the company's dedication to data protection, the CEO speaks with the media.

Consistency and Coordination: Make sure all communication channels are using the same messaging to prevent misunderstandings or contradicting facts. To guarantee message coherence and alignment, schedule internal and external communications.

To keep the narrative in control, assign a spokesperson or team to respond to questions from the media and make public remarks.

Example: A pharmaceutical business will, in the event of a product recall, send out news releases, social media posts, and a consistent message on its website outlining the reasons behind the recall, any possible risks, and consumer instructions.

Press briefings are held by the company's official spokesman to address inquiries and provide updates to reporters.

Adaptability and Flexibility: Continue to be adaptable and flexible in the face of changing circumstances and fresh knowledge. As objectives change and feedback and stakeholder reactions come in, make necessary adjustments to communication strategies and techniques.

Make necessary revisions after regularly assessing the success of crisis communication initiatives.

Example: A contentious policy decision has sparked resentment from members of a hospitality industry association. The association's crisis communication team responds by calling an emergency meeting to reevaluate its strategy and chooses to make public an apology and amend the policy in light of member input.

To regain consensus and confidence, they consult stakeholders and convey the changes in an open and transparent manner. In conclusion, following the criteria that sees readiness, transparency, consistency, adaptability, and collaboration as a priority is necessary for creating efficient crisis communication plans and handling emergencies.

By following these guidelines and leveraging real-world examples, organisations can effectively manage crises and protect their reputation and stakeholders' trust.

Top 3 Frustrations in Crisis Communication

- **Lack of Preparedness:** Many organisations and individuals feel unprepared when a crisis hits, resulting in confusion and ineffective communication. This leads to mismanagement of information, inconsistent messaging, and increased anxiety among stakeholders.
- **Misinformation and Rumours**: The spread of misinformation and rumours can quickly escalate during a crisis, making it difficult to control the narrative. This

creates panic, damages credibility, and complicates communication efforts.

- **Speed of Response:** The need to respond quickly to a crisis can overwhelm communicators, leading to rushed and potentially flawed messages. Delays or mistakes in communication can exacerbate the crisis and erode trust.

Top 3 Fears in Crisis Communication

- **Fear of Making the Situation Worse:** Communicators often fear that their words or actions might inadvertently escalate the crisis. This fear can lead to hesitation or overly cautious communication, delaying necessary responses.
- **Fear of Public Scrutiny and Backlash:** The fear of negative public reaction or backlash can be paralysing for those handling crisis communication. This can result in a lack of transparency or defensive communication, further damaging reputation.
- **Fear of Inadequate Communication Skills:** Individuals may doubt their ability to communicate effectively under pressure, fearing they might not convey the right message. This self-doubt can undermine confidence and lead to less effective communication.

Top 3 Ways to Overcome Crisis Communication Challenges

- **Develop a Crisis Communication Plan:** Prepare a comprehensive crisis communication plan that includes roles, protocols, and messaging templates. Having a plan in place ensures a quick, organised, and consistent response, reducing confusion and enhancing confidence.

- **Train and Practice Regularly:** Conduct regular training sessions and simulations for all potential communicators to practice crisis scenarios. Training helps build skills, confidence, and familiarity with the crisis communication plan, making actual responses more effective.
- **Establish Clear Communication Channels:** Identify and utilise clear, reliable communication channels to disseminate information quickly and accurately. Clear channels prevent the spread of misinformation, ensure timely updates, and maintain stakeholder trust.

10

The Future of Communication

Human contact and societal advancement are fundamentally based on communication. The means and channels by which we communicate have changed continuously from the first languages to the digital era.

Looking ahead, a number of significant developments are reshaping communication in ways that will affect how we interact, exchange information, and create connections.

VR and Augmented Reality (AR): Through the creation of immersive experiences that go beyond physical bounds, virtual reality and augmented reality technologies have the potential to completely transform communication. In the future, people may engage with one another as though they were in the same room when attending meetings, seminars, or social events in virtual worlds. For instance, businesses may hold online product demos or training sessions, enabling users to interact with the material more deeply.

AI: AI-powered communication solutions are getting more advanced, allowing for more simplified workflows and customised interactions. Virtual assistants and chatbots can already respond to simple consumer requests, but in the future, they might be able to grasp context, tone, and emotion just like humans. This could lead to better customer service encounters and more effective communication across a range of industries.

5G Technology: As 5G networks are deployed, quicker and more dependable connectivity will be possible, facilitating real-time interactions and assisting in the growth of Internet of Things (IoT) devices. 5G will enable seamless data flow, resulting in smoother and more immersive applications like gaming, video streaming, and remote collaboration. It will also offer more bandwidth and lower latency.

Voice Technology: With its hands-free capabilities and user-friendly interfaces, voice-activated gadgets and services are becoming more and more common. Voice technology may advance to the point where it can smoothly accommodate user choices and comprehend natural language with more accuracy in the future. This might change the way we use our gadgets, from web searches to managing smart home automation.

Blockchain: Although blockchain is most commonly associated with cryptocurrency, it also has potential applications in secure and open communication. Blockchain enables verifiable information transmission and trustless transactions by decentralising data storage and guaranteeing cryptographic security. Communication platforms built on blockchain technology may one day enable people to take control of their online privacy and digital identities.

Multimodal Communication: People are choosing to express themselves more and more through several modalities as communication outlets proliferate.

A vital component of internet chats, emoticons, GIFs, and memes convey emotions and increase participation. Through the seamless integration of text, images, videos, and virtual elements, multimodal communication advances may eventually result in more expressive and immersive interactions.

Cultural and Linguistic Diversity: Technology developments and globalisation have made it possible for communication to be more culturally and linguistically diverse. This tendency is probably going to continue in the future, which will result in the creation of inclusive communication methods and tools. With the advancement of translation technologies, linguistic barriers will be eliminated, and intercultural understanding will be promoted globally.

Ethical and Legal Considerations: The legal and ethical consequences of communication technology use also change as they advance. A lot more thought and legislation will be needed for issues like digital rights, privacy, and data security as they get more complicated. Assuring that communication technologies serve the public good will require future stakeholders to work together to create frameworks that strike a balance between innovation and accountability.

Education and Empowerment: In order to participate in the digital age, one must have access to communication technology. In order to empower people and communities in the future, efforts to close the digital divide and advance digital literacy will be essential. In order to equip people to appropriately traverse the intricacies of the digital ecosystem, education systems will need to adapt in order to teach critical thinking, media literacy, and online etiquette, among other vital communication skills.

Socioeconomic Impact: Future communication will shape economies, civilisations, and industries with significant socioeconomic ramifications. Communication technology will completely change the way we live, work, and communicate with each other.

Examples include e-commerce, social activism, remote work and telemedicine. To make sure that the advantages of technological innovation are shared fairly, it is crucial to foresee and reduce any potential discrepancies.

In summary, the future of communication is incredibly promising and will be shaped by societal change, technological advancement, and cultural evolution. We may use communication to create a more open, successful, and connected society by embracing new trends and tackling related issues.

The communication landscape is always changing due to emerging trends and technology, which are revolutionising the ways in which people and organisations connect, communicate, and exchange information.

Here's an in-depth exploration of these transformative forces, along with examples illustrating their impact:

5G Technology: The introduction of 5G networks offers unprecedented connection, reduced latency, and rapid data rates. By facilitating smooth communication amongst gadgets, this technology opens the door for developments in the IoT, AR, and VR applications.

For instance, healthcare providers can diagnose and treat patients in real-time, no matter how far away they are, by using high-definition video conversations over 5G networks to perform remote medical consultations.

AI in Communication: Communication channels are being revolutionised by AI-powered chatbots, virtual assistants, and language translation technologies.

These AI-powered solutions simplify repetitive processes, improve customer service, and enable multilingual communication. Businesses such as Google and Microsoft, for instance, have created AI-powered translation services that translate speech and text in a variety of languages instantaneously, facilitating easy communication between people with disparate linguistic backgrounds.

Voice Technology: AI-powered virtual assistants, like Google Assistant, Apple's Siri, and Amazon's Alexa, are finding their way into daily conversations. Voice commands are supported for controlling smart home devices and retrieving information from these devices. Further enhancing the user experience is the ability to recognise and comprehend voice messages more accurately, thanks to developments in natural language processing (NLP).

AR and VR: Through the creation of immersive and interactive experiences, AR and VR technologies are revolutionising communication. AR applications, for example, improve real-time communication and collaboration by superimposing digital information onto the real world. Conversely, VR facilitates user interaction with virtual settings, allowing for distant meetings, training sessions, and virtual events.

Blockchain Technology: Although blockchain is most recognised for its use in cryptocurrency, it is also being investigated for use in transparent and safe communication networks.

Blockchain-based systems provide decentralised file-sharing and messaging while protecting privacy and data integrity. One illustration is the emergence of decentralised social media platforms, which remove the need for middlemen and lower the danger of data breaches by giving users complete control over their data and privacy settings.

IoT: As IoT devices proliferate, they are connecting ecosystems in which devices may easily exchange data and communicate with one another.

Data collection, processing, and sharing are being revolutionised by IoT technology, which is found in everything from wearables and smart homes to industrial sensors and self-driving cars. IoT-enabled smart cities, for instance, use sensor networks to keep an eye on traffic patterns, maximise energy use, and improve public safety—all of which contribute to increased efficiency and communication within the city.

Extended Reality (XR): VR, AR, and mixed reality (MR) are all included in XR, which provides engaging and immersive experiences in a range of sectors. XR technologies facilitate virtual meetings, team-based design sessions, and immersive marketing campaigns in the communication domain.

In contrast to conventional techniques, XR technologies enable architects and designers to visualise and convey design concepts to clients in a way that is more interesting and perceptive.

Data Analytics and Personalization: Organizations can study enormous volumes of communication data to gain insightful knowledge and customise interactions by using advanced data analytics tools. Social media companies, for instance, employ machine learning algorithms to evaluate user activity and preferences in order to present tailored content and adverts depending on users' interests and demographics.

Quantum Communication: Secure and unbreakable communication channels are made possible by quantum communication, which makes use of the ideas of quantum physics.

Unmatched levels of security are provided by quantum encryption techniques like quantum key distribution (QKD), which make it nearly impossible for unauthorized parties to intercept or decipher transmitted data. Places like government organisations, financial institutions, and healthcare providers that require extremely secure communication have a lot of potential when it comes to quantum communication.

Biometric Authentication: Communication systems and devices are increasingly using biometric identification techniques, including voice, facial, and fingerprint recognition.

By improving security and streamlining user authentication procedures, these authentication techniques lessen the need for conventional passwords and PINs.

For instance, cell phones with facial recognition software enable users to authenticate transactions and unlock their devices using facial biometrics, providing a safe and convenient means of communication.

These new developments in technology and trends are transforming communication in the future, spurring innovation, and opening up new avenues for participation, connectivity, and cooperation across a range of industries.

These technologies will surely become increasingly important in determining how we connect and communicate in the years to come as they develop further. The transmission of emotions and information between people, known as interpersonal communication, is changing dramatically as a result of advances in VR, AI, and other cutting-edge technology.

Not only are these technologies altering the way we communicate with one another, but they are also transforming the very essence of human interaction. Let's take a look at few of those ways.

Language Translation: AI-powered language translation technologies enable communication between speakers of different languages by removing linguistic barriers. This encourages worldwide cooperation and understanding across cultural boundaries.

AI systems are capable of accurately recognising and interpreting emotions by analysing non-verbal clues such as tone of voice and facial expressions.

Emotion Recognition: AI systems are capable of accurately identifying and interpreting emotions by analysing non-verbal clues such as tone of voice and facial expressions. This makes it possible for people to communicate more empathetically by improving their understanding of one another's emotions, even during virtual exchanges.

Content Generation: Social media postings, videos, and articles produced by AI have the power to spark conversations and build relationships among people who have similar interests. However, if AI-generated content is not adequately regulated, worries about disinformation and manipulation can surface.

VR: Virtual reality technology builds surroundings that are so realistic that people can communicate with one another virtually, even if they are physically far apart. Deeper relationships result from an increased sense of closeness and presence in communication.

Virtual Meetings and Collaboration: By simulating in-person interactions, VR-enabled meetings and collaborative platforms facilitate more organic and effective communication among participants. This encourages greater collaboration and creativity while lowering the constraints of conventional video conferencing.

Building Empathy: VR experiences can submerge people in made-up situations that encourage empathy and an appreciation for various viewpoints. People can improve their empathy and communication abilities and have more meaningful interactions in real life by digitally putting themselves in other people's shoes.

Virtual Social Spaces: VR social platforms offer virtual environments where people can socialise, attend events, and engage in recreational activities together. These platforms provide opportunities for spontaneous interactions and serendipitous connections, similar to real-world social settings.

Other Innovations: AR improves in-person interactions and experiences by superimposing digital data over the real world. AR-enabled communication tools can facilitate cooperative problem-solving in a variety of scenarios, enhance navigation, and supply contextual information.

Biometric Sensors: During communication, wearable biometric sensors can monitor physiological signs including skin conductance, heart rate, and brain activity. By improving self-awareness and emotional control, these biofeedback data can improve interpersonal communication.

Brain-Computer Interfaces (BCIs): Bypassing conventional sensory-motor pathways, BCIs allow direct brain-to-external device connection. BCIs have the potential to transform communication for people with impairments and open the door to new forms of telepathic communication in the future, even if they are still in the early phases of development.

In conclusion, cutting-edge technology like virtual reality, artificial intelligence, and others are fundamentally changing interpersonal communication. While there are many advantages to these developments, like more individualised communication, immersive experiences, and the development of empathy, there are also moral, privacy, and legal issues that need to be resolved. We must encourage the prudent use of these technologies as we continue to incorporate them into our daily lives and make sure that they complement real human connection rather than take its place.

Evolving Communication Skills: Navigating the Ever-Changing Landscape of Human Interaction

The world is changing so quickly that having good communication skills is more important than ever. Technology breakthroughs, globalisation, and shifting social standards have caused a steady shift in the way we interact.

In order to prosper in an ever-changing setting, people need to modify and advance their communication abilities. They may successfully negotiate the complexity of modern interaction by accepting change and always improving their skills.

The emergence of digital communication platforms is a key factor in the need to adjust communication abilities. The emergence of messaging applications, social media, and virtual meetings in recent years has completely changed how people communicate and engage. In order to interact with people in this digital world, people need to become proficient in the skill of communicating in a clear and powerful way.

Effective internet communication is essential, whether you're sending out a compelling video conference presentation, writing a formal email, or creating an interesting tweet. Furthermore, as a result of globalisation, borders between countries have become less distinct, resulting in different workplaces and communities. People working in such settings need to be highly skilled in verbal communication in addition to having empathy and cultural awareness.

Building lasting relationships and promoting cross-border collaboration requires an understanding of cultural nuances, respect for diversity, and the ability to modify communication approaches accordingly. In addition, new platforms and tools for communication have emerged as a result of the quick speed at which technology is developing.

These technologies, which range from artificial intelligence to machine learning, from virtual reality to augmented reality, are changing how we connect and communicate. In order to remain current and competitive, people need to know these advancements and learn how to leverage them to enhance their communication effectiveness.

Apart from the progress made in technology, shifts in society are also impacting communication patterns. An increasing number of people are using more inclusive language and communication techniques as a result of the growing emphasis on diversity, equity, and inclusion.

People need to be aware of the language they use, try to steer clear of prejudice and preconceptions, and work to build inclusive settings where everyone is treated with respect and value.

Furthermore, the prevalence of remote work, accelerated by the COVID-19 pandemic, has highlighted the importance of effective online communication. As more businesses adopt remote work policies and flexible schedules, individuals must adapt to communicating efficiently in virtual environments to maintain productivity and collaboration.

This entails learning the proper approach to conducting video conferences, making use of collaboration technologies, and coming up with inventive ways to keep team members motivated and cohesive even when they are physically apart.

Furthermore, the prevalence of remote work has brought attention to how important it is to maintain effective communication and collaboration among team members, ensuring that productivity and morale remain high despite physical distance.

In a virtual setting where in-person interactions are scarce, miscommunication can quickly occur if instructions are not clear and comprehensive.

To guarantee mutual comprehension, people must thus develop good written communication skills, make sure their messages are clear, and actively seek out feedback.

In addition, soft skills like empathy, creativity, and communication are becoming more and more important as automation and artificial intelligence continue to change the nature of work.

Even while robotic systems are highly proficient in carrying out monotonous duties, they are unable to fully substitute human contact in intricate interpersonal situations.

To be competitive in the employment market of the future, people must therefore concentrate on enhancing and developing their special human qualities.

Furthermore, both professional and personal development depend on having strong communication abilities.

Whether it's haggling over pay, dealing with a conflict, or networking with peers, the ability to communicate persuasively and assertively can open doors to new opportunities and advancement.

By improving their communication abilities, people can become more capable leaders, forge closer bonds with others, and accomplish their objectives more successfully.

In conclusion, good communication is more crucial than ever in a world that is always evolving due to globalisation, technological advancement, and shifting social standards.

People can prosper in today's environment of interpersonal communication by accepting change, adjusting to new technologies, and developing excellent communication skills.

Learning how to communicate effectively is an ongoing process that involves developing interpersonal skills, accepting cultural diversity, and navigating online communication platforms. Individuals can position themselves for success in both their personal and professional lives by making a commitment to lifelong learning and evolution.

How Do You Plan to Become a Better Communicator?

List the Hacks You Think Have Helped You the Most

About the Author

Deesha Sangani is a Bangalore-based Author, Certified Communication Coach, and Motivational Speaker. Known for her transformative insights on communication, she empowers individuals to elevate their personal and professional interactions.

With a passion for helping others unlock their potential, Deesha continues to inspire through her writing and speaking engagements. She is also a highly influential blogger, an inspiration for many who want to live their dreams whilst following a corporate career.